ECDL® 5.0

European Computer Driving Licence

Module 2 - IT User Fundamentals
using Windows 7

This training, which has been approved by ECDL Foundation, includes exercise items intended to assist Candidates in their training for an ECDL Certification Programme. These exercises are not ECDL Foundation certification tests. For information about authorised Test Centres in different national territories, please refer to the ECDL Foundation website at www.ecdl.org

Release BSC014v2

Module 2 IT User Fundamentals   ECDL/ICDL 5.0

Published by:

> CiA Training Ltd
> Business & Innovation Centre
> Sunderland Enterprise Park
> Sunderland SR5 2TA
> United Kingdom
>
> Tel: +44 (0) 191 549 5002
> Fax: +44 (0) 191 549 9005
>
> E-mail: info@ciatraining.co.uk
> Web: www.ciatraining.co.uk
>
> **ISBN-13: 978 1 86005 842 4**

First published 2010

Copyright © 2010 CiA Training Ltd

All rights reserved. No part of this publication may be reproduced, stored in a retrieval system, or transmitted in any form or by any means (electronic, mechanical, photocopying, recording or otherwise) without the prior written permission of CiA Training Limited.

Microsoft is a registered trademark and Windows is a trademark of the Microsoft Corporation. Screen images reproduced by permission of the Microsoft Corporation. All other trademarks in this book are acknowledged as the property of their respective owners.

ECDL/ICDL 5.0   ***Module 2 IT User Fundamentals***

ECDL Foundation
Approved Courseware

Downloading the Data Files

The data associated with these exercises must be downloaded from our website. Go to: *www.ciatraining.co.uk/data*. Follow the on screen instructions to download the **Windows 7** data files, if not previously downloaded.

By default, the data files will be downloaded to **CIA DATA FILES\ECDL\2 Managing Files** in the **Documents** library.

If you prefer, the data can be supplied on CD at an additional cost. Contact the Sales team at *info@ciatraining.co.uk*.

Aims

To familiarise the user with the main operating features of *Windows Vista,* the **Desktop**, application windows and display settings. To demonstrate the ability to manage files and organise folders. Use a word processing application and understand the basic operations associated with creating and editing a word processed document. To understand the importance of maintenance of IT systems and how to tackle common problems. To be aware of security issues and laws and guidance covering the use of IT.

Objectives

After completing the guide the user will be able to:

- Use the main features of the operating system, including adjusting the main computer settings and using built-in help features

- Operate effectively around the computer desktop and work effectively in a graphical user environment

- Know about the main concepts of file management and be able to efficiently organise files and folders so that they are easy to identify and find

- Use utility software to compress and extract large files and use anti-virus software to protect against computer viruses

- Demonstrate the ability to use simple text editing and print tools available within the operating system

Assessment of Knowledge

At the end of this guide is a section called the **Record of Achievement Matrix**. Before the guide is started it is recommended that the user complete the matrix to measure the level of current knowledge.

Tick boxes are provided for each feature. **1** is for no knowledge, **2** some knowledge and **3** is for competent.

After working through a section, complete the **Record of Achievement** matrix for that section and only when competent in all areas move on to the next section.

Contents

Section 1
Getting Started

By the end of this Section you should be able to:

Appreciate Health & Safety and Legal Issues

Start, Restart and Close Down the Computer

Identify Parts of a Window

Understand Start Menu and Taskbar

Recognise and Arrange Desktop Icons

Open, Resize and Close Windows

View System Properties

Use Help

To gain an understanding of the above features, work through the **Driving Lessons** in this **Section**.

For each **Driving Lesson**, read the **Park and Read** instructions, without touching the keyboard, then work through the numbered steps of the **Manoeuvres** on the computer. Complete the **Revision Exercise(s)** at the end of the section to test your knowledge.

Driving Lesson 1 - Preparation

▣ Park and Read

Health and Safety

Before you turn a computer on, you have to make sure you will be able to use it safely; this means safe for you as a user and safe for other people. Your work station must conform to the relevant Health and Safety at Work (HASAW) legislation. A workplace that has swivel chairs with adjustable positions, stable, roomy desks, etc., will provide a working environment that is comfortable and safe. Furniture and equipment should be suitably positioned and conform to any necessary regulations. It should be arranged carefully to prevent accidents within this environment. Injuries common in an IT environment are:

- Aches and pains due to bad posture when seated for long periods
- Repetitive strain injury (RSI) caused by poor position of the seat/desk combined with repeated movements of the same joints over a long period of time
- Paper cuts from refilling printers/photocopiers
- Eye strain which can be caused by glare or flickering from a VDU and by not taking regular visual breaks (10 minutes every hour is recommended) away from the screen
- Electric shocks due to incorrect working practice or dangerous wiring
- Injuries due to tripping over trailing wires or other obstructions.

ℹ️ *See **Driving Lesson 69 Health and Safety** for further information.*

Laws and Guidelines

There are many rules and regulations that affect how you use IT on a daily basis. You need to be aware of these and consider how they affect you personally.

Data Protection

The Data Protection Act (1998) regulates the use of personal data by all businesses. Personal data is any data that can be used to identify a living individual; it includes names, addresses, personalised e-mail addresses and video images of such individuals.

Basically, any type of business, financial institution, dentist, doctor or local authority that can identify a living individual by the information they hold, is covered by the Data Protection Act. In the workplace, a manager has to make sure this type of data is used in the right way. When information is held about individuals, the manager must ensure that the data is accurate and that the individuals are aware that this information is being kept.

continued over

Driving Lesson 1 - Continued

Copyright

The effect of copyright on the day to day use of IT is that any text or picture scanned into a PC and saved, any graphic image, text file, audio or video file downloaded from the Internet and saved to disk is illegal, unless specifically identified by its owner as being copyright-free. This also applies to any digital material saved to any storage device.

See **Driving Lesson 73 Copyright** *for further information.*

Equal Opportunities

You must conform to equal opportunities guidelines by making sure that nothing you produce could be offensive to those viewing it on grounds of gender, ethnic origin, religion, sexual orientation or disability.

Disability

There are also laws to ensure that people with disabilities are able to use IT in the same way as those without disabilities. This may mean the provision of specially adapted hardware such as mice, or software such as screen readers, voice recognition or magnifiers. This can also affect what you produce, for example web pages - these must be accessible to people with disabilities and there are certain standards that should be followed. The World Wide Web Consortium (W3C) develops and maintains web standards, which include the WAI - Web Accessibility Initiative.

Manoeuvres

1.   Think about how the legal issues mentioned above apply to you at work.

2.   Make sure your chair is at the correct height and angle so that you can sit comfortably at the computer. Your feet should be flat on the floor and your back should be straight.

3.   Make sure that you can see the screen properly and that there is no glare. You can change the angle of the monitor if necessary.

4.   When you are entirely comfortable, move on to the next exercise.

Driving Lesson 2 - Starting the Computer

P Park and Read

A computer consists of various parts: a processing unit, keyboard, monitor, mouse and, optionally, a printer. The processing unit is switched on to start the computer. When the computer has started up, you may be required to log on to identify yourself to the system. For security reasons this is done using a user name and password.

Manoeuvres

1.   Before switching a computer on:

- check for lights, usually green, on the front of the computer which shows that it is already on. If there is a light on but the screen is blank, the computer is in a dormant state; either move the mouse or press a key on the keyboard.

- check the floppy drive (if present) and the CD drive for disks. Some computers are set to try and start directly from a floppy or CD if there is one present. If there is a disk in either drive, remove it.

CD drive

USB Ports

On/Off Switch

Case contains Processing Unit

Monitor

Keyboard

Mouse

continued over

Driving Lesson 2 - Continued

2.   Press the **Power Switch** on the front of the computer (some computers may have the power switch at the back).

3.   If the monitor power light does not come on, press the monitor power button (some monitors take their power from the computer unit).

4.   When both units are powered the computer goes through a startup routine and displays information on the screen.

5.   After various checks the *Windows* operating system is loaded.

6.   *Windows 7* allows more than one user to sign on to the same computer and maintain their own profile. If there are multiple users the screen shows icons for every available user defined on this computer and allows the correct profile to be selected.

7.   Click your user name or icon to start *Windows* with your profile active.

8.   If your account is password protected, you will be prompted for the password now. If you are connected to a network you may be prompted for a different **User name** and **Password**.

9.   The *Windows* **Desktop** screen is displayed.

Driving Lesson 3 - The Windows Desktop

▣ Park and Read

The **Desktop** may be customised according to the user's preference; every aspect of its appearance can be changed. For example, the general style of the screens can be set to **Classic** (to resemble previous Windows versions) and often a picture is used as the background image. For this reason**, _the screens shown in this guide may not match that of your computer_**. The basic layout, however, should be the same.

⌒ Manoeuvres

1.   The screen shows the **Desktop**. This is the starting point for all tasks performed in *Windows*. From here it is possible to control the operation of the computer, access all programs, and perform file management tasks.

2.   The screen is similar to that shown below, although some icons have been added. The **Desktop** for a new system will have only a **Taskbar** and a **Recycle Bin**.

3.   Along the bottom of the **Desktop** screen is a bar known as the **Taskbar**. This is used as a quick way to access certain features. This bar usually remains on screen at all times. At the right of the screen it is possible to add a variety of **Gadgets**.

4.   The icons (small graphics with text underneath) in the main part of the screen represent objects saved on the **Desktop** or shortcuts that lead directly to a program, folder, file, etc.

continued over

Driving Lesson 3 - Continued

5. Some examples of common desktop icons are listed below. These will be covered in more detail in later exercises.

Recycle Bin	The **Recycle Bin** is a location where deleted items are placed
Microsoft Word 2010	This is a shortcut pointer to an application (Word). Double click it to start the application.
Development Folders2 -	This is a shortcut pointer to a folder Double click it to display the contents of the folder.
Budget	This represents a file stored on the desktop. Double click it to open the file in the appropriate application.
HP LaserJet P2015 Series	This is a shortcut to a printer. Double click it to open the printer window for this device.

6. Some of these, and other icons, ay also appear in other views such as when displaying the Computer or Documents windows. These are also covered later.

Local Disk (C:)	This is an icon for a device in the computer, in this case the local hard disk drive.
CIA DATA FILES	This is an icon for a folder.
Database1	This is an icon for a file in a folder, in this case an *Access* database file

Driving Lesson 4 - Arranging Icons

▣ Park and Read

Icons on the **Desktop** can be arranged into any suitable order.

Nearly all *Windows* tasks can be performed using the mouse. There are a few different mouse techniques, they are:

Point	*position the mouse pointer until the tip of the pointer rests on the required position*
Click	*press and immediately release the left mouse button without moving the mouse*
Right Click	*press and immediately release the right mouse button without moving the mouse*
Double click	*click the left mouse button twice in rapid succession without moving the mouse*
Drag	*press the left mouse button and hold it down while the mouse is moved, then release the button at the appropriate location*

ℹ️ *Unless otherwise stated, when instructed to click, use the left mouse button.*

ℹ️ *It is possible to have a 'left handed' mouse configuration in which the left and right mouse buttons are reversed.*

Icons in any window, or on the **Desktop**, can be clicked and dragged to any position required. They will then stay in position until moved again.

⌕ Manoeuvres

1. Move the mouse around the desk. The mouse pointer will move around the screen, in the direction of the mouse movement.

2. Move the mouse pointer over one of the icons on the screen, such as the **Recycle Bin** icon, a background appears around the icon. An information label is displayed, explaining the feature. Click once and the background lightens, showing the icon is selected.

3. Move the mouse pointer to a clear part of the **Desktop** and click to deselect the icon.

4. Move the mouse pointer over a blank part of the **Desktop** and click once with the **right** mouse button. A **Shortcut Menu** is displayed. If there is an arrow at the right of some options, such as the **View** option, this indicates there are further choices available.

continued over

Driving Lesson 4 - Continued

5.   Without clicking, place the mouse pointer over **View**. A secondary menu is displayed. If **Auto arrange icons** is ticked, then click on **Auto arrange icons** to turn it off (**Auto arrange icons** keeps the icons in place on the left, so they cannot be moved). If not, click anywhere on the **Desktop** away from the menus.

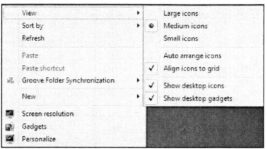

6.   With **Auto arrange icons** turned off the icons can be moved around. Click on any icon and hold the mouse button down. Drag the icon around the screen by moving the mouse, release the mouse button.

7.   Move the icon back to its original position.

8.   By clicking and dragging, move some of the icons around the **Desktop**. If only one icon is present on the **Desktop** then read the rest of this exercise for information and carry on with the next Driving Lesson.

9.   Click with the **right** mouse button again and use the **View** menu to switch on the **Auto arrange icons** option.

10.   Click with the **right** mouse button again, select **Sort by** option and then **Name**. The icons on the **Desktop** are now arranged neatly in name order (although some system icons may always be shown first).

    *If no new shortcut icons have been created on the **Desktop**, **Sort by** may have no effect as they may be already arranged by name.*

11.   Click with the **right** mouse button again and select **Sort by**, then **Size** from the secondary menu. The icons are now arranged with the largest file first (useful if there are many objects stored on the **Desktop**).

12.   Rearrange the icons by **Item type**. This is the default.

13.   Click with the **right** mouse button and select **View**, then **Large icons**. The icons now appear much larger.

14.   Click with the **right** mouse button and select **View**, then **Small icons**. The icons now appear smaller, as they did in earlier *Windows* versions.

15.   Click with the **right** mouse button and select **View**, then **Medium icons**. This is the default view.

Driving Lesson 5 - The Taskbar

▣ Park and Read

The **Taskbar** is displayed across the bottom of the screen. The **Start** button is on the left. Some **Quick Launch** buttons may be displayed to the right of this. The buttons seen on the **Taskbar** depend on which options have been selected.

More than one program may run at the same time (multi-tasking). As each program is started, a button appears on the **Taskbar** as an icon (the program's name is not displayed by default).

The **Taskbar** button for the **active** program, i.e. the one that is currently being used, appears lighter.

☞ Manoeuvres

1. Look at the buttons at the left of the **Taskbar**. Move the cursor over them and read the associated **Tooltip** for each one. Icons can be pinned to the **Taskbar**. This keeps the program icon permanently on the **Taskbar**.

2. The centre part of the **Taskbar** is blank at the moment but is used to display program buttons (covered later).

3. Move the cursor slowly over the icons at the right of the **Taskbar** (the **Notification Area**) to see the tooltips. These may include the **Date/Time** and **Volume** controls if they have been set up. These are covered later.

4. To move or resize the **Taskbar**, it must be unlocked. Right click on an unoccupied area on the **Taskbar** and click **Lock the taskbar** to remove the check and unlock the bar.

5. Point to any unoccupied area on the **Taskbar**, then click and drag to the right of the screen. Move the **Taskbar** to the left of the screen and then drag it back to its original position at the bottom.

6. Move the mouse pointer slowly over the upper edge of the **Taskbar**. The mouse pointer will change shape into a double-headed arrow, ⬍. Click and drag this **Adjust** cursor up slightly to double the size of the **Taskbar** (useful if many programs are open).

7. Reduce the size of the **Taskbar** to its default size, i.e. one line.

8. Lock the **Taskbar** again by right clicking on it and selecting **Lock the taskbar**.

Driving Lesson 6 - The Start Menu

▣ Park and Read

At the left of the **Taskbar**, is the **Start** button, ⬤. This button is used to start any program that is loaded on the computer and has been included in the menus.

↱ Manoeuvres

1.   Click on the **Start** button to display the **Start** menu.

Application Icons

    Getting Started
    Calculator
    Connect to a Projector
    Sticky Notes
    Paint Shop Pro 4
    Paint
    Snipping Tool
    XPS Viewer
    Windows Fax and Scan
    Remote Desktop Connection
    ▶ All Programs
    Search programs and files

    Ian Chapman
    Documents
    Pictures
    Music
    Computer
    Control Panel
    Devices and Printers
    Default Programs
    Help and Support
    Shut down

2.   The **Start** menu has two areas. At the left are common and recently used programs, which will vary as different programs are used, and at the right are the permanent **Start** options, which will vary depending on how *Windows* has been installed.

continued over

Driving Lesson 6 - Continued

3. The fixed **Start** menu options will vary with the version of *Windows* installed. Some of the main ones are:

User Name (Ian Chapman)	*opens the main folder for this user.*
Documents	*opens the **Documents** library for the current user.*
Pictures	*opens the **Pictures** folder for the current user.*
Music	*opens the **Music** folder for the current user.*
Computer	*gives access to drives and hardware on your computer.*
Control Panel	*allows control over the settings and options for all hardware and software on the computer.*
Devices and Printers	*adds devices and printers.*
Default Programs	*choose programs that Windows uses by default.*
Help and Support	*gives access to the Windows **Help** system.*
Shut Down	*options to close down the computer.*

4. Move the cursor over the **All Programs** option at the lower left of the start menu, which gives access to all programs on your computer. A list of available programs will appear. Any program can be started by clicking on it.

5. Some programs are grouped into folders. Click on the **Accessories** folder, to display its contents.

continued over

Driving Lesson 6 - Continued

6. Programs such as **Notepad** or **Paint** can be started by clicking from this list.

7. There can be further structure in the **All Programs** list. Look down the list of programs in **Accessories** and click on the **System Tools** folder.

i *You may have to **scroll** down the list by clicking the down arrow at the right of the list. Scrolling is covered in a later Driving Lesson.*

8. This folder contains programs that help to control and configure the systems on your computer. Press the **Escape <Esc>** key on the keyboard to return to the main **Start** menu.

9. Click once on any blank part of the **Desktop** to cancel the **Start** menu and return to the **Desktop** display.

Driving Lesson 7 - Opening Windows

▣ Park and Read

Windows are rectangular areas of the screen in which programs are run, or system data is presented. All windows have similar properties although there are differences between the two types mentioned above. Many windows can be open at a time, each performing a different task.

☞ Manoeuvres

1. Click **Start** and click on **Computer** from the right of the **Start** menu.

2. The **Computer** window will open. This is an example of a system window, although some icons may be different to those shown below.

3. The appearance of the window will depend on which options are set. Click the **Organize** button on the toolbar and select **Layout**. Make sure the **Menu bar** option is selected (with a tick), and the **Details pane** and **Navigation pane** are also selected in order to obtain the picture below.

✓	Menu bar
✓	Details pane
☐	Preview pane
✓	Navigation pane

    They may not be on by default. The **Menu bar** may be switched off later if required.

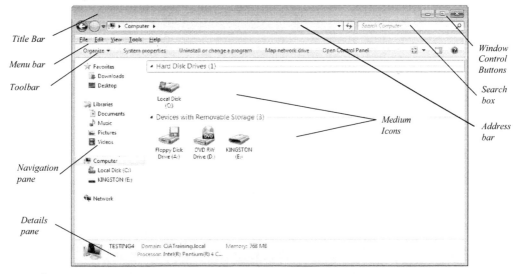

4. Each window is similar in its construction. A **Title Bar** is across the top, (although this window has no title) with three **Window Control Buttons** at the right. These are **Minimize**, ⬚, **Maximize**, ⬚, and **Close**, ⬚.

continued over

Driving Lesson 7 - Continued

5. If the window fills the whole screen, the **Maximize** button is replaced by the **Restore Down** button in the centre of the **Window Control Buttons**. If the **Restore Down** button is displayed, click it now to reduce the size of the window.

6. The **Maximize** button increases the size of the window to its maximum size, probably filling the screen. Click the **Maximize** button of the **Computer** window.

7. The **Maximize** button is replaced by the **Restore Down** button, . Click the **Restore Down** button to change the maximised window back to its previous size.

8. The **Minimize** button hides the window completely. Click the **Minimize** button of the **Computer** window.

9. When a window is minimised, the program or task in the window is not ended and its button is still displayed on the **Taskbar** as active, . Place the cursor over the button, the **Tooltip** displays **Computer**, the window that is minimized. Click the **Computer** icon on the **Taskbar** to redisplay the window, then use the **Maximize** button to expand it.

10. Below the **Title Bar** is an **Address bar** to show where you are looking. Some windows have **Back** and **Forward** buttons at the left of this bar and a **Search box** to allow you to search within the current window.

11. Below the **Address Bar** is the **Menu bar**. Click on a menu and view the attached list. Note that some of the items may be ghosted, greyed out, this means that they are not available under the present circumstances. Move the mouse pointer along the **Menu bar** to display the other lists.

12. Click on the selected menu again or click on any blank part of the window to remove the menu.

13. Below the **Menu bar** is the **Toolbar**. This is a row of named buttons to quickly achieve tasks without using the menu alternative. Move the mouse over one of these. A **ToolTip** will appear, giving a description of its function or sometimes only the button name.

i *The window for a program or application is slightly different. There is always a name in the Title Bar, the Menu bar is always present, but the Toolbar may be missing. For more information see the section on Running Applications.*

i *Office 2007 application windows are different again with the Menu bar and Toolbar replaced by a variable Ribbon area.*

14. Use the button to restore the **Computer** window to its previous size.

Driving Lesson 8 - Sizing and Moving Windows

▣ Park and Read

If a window is not maximised (filling the whole screen), the size and position of it can be changed.

↱ Manoeuvres

1. Move the mouse pointer over the **Title Bar** of the **Computer** window.

2. Click and drag downwards. The entire window will move down, be careful not to move any part of the window off the screen. Release the mouse button.

3. The size of the window can be changed. Move the mouse pointer over the right edge of the window, until the pointer changes to a double headed arrow.

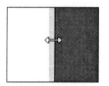

4. Click and drag to the right, and then release the mouse button, to increase the width of the window.

5. Placing the mouse over a corner of a window allows the size of a window to be changed in two directions at once, maintaining the overall shape, e.g. a square will remain a square. Place the mouse pointer over the bottom right corner of the **Computer** window so that it changes to a two headed diagonal arrow.

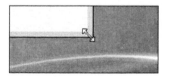

6. Click and drag a small amount in any direction to change the size and scale of the window.

Driving Lesson 9 - Close a Window

▣ Park and Read

The **Close** button, , at the top right of every window, closes it and any process being performed within it. If there is a process running in a window there may be a warning message before closing.

⌒ Manoeuvres

1. Click the **Close** button, ▐X▌, in the top right of the **Computer** window. The window is closed. The **Computer** icon on the **Taskbar** is no longer highlighted (not active) and its description changes to **Windows Explorer**.

2. Click **Start** and select **All Programs** from the **Start** menu.

3. Open the **Accessories** folder and click on 🎨 Paint   to start the **Paint** application in a new window.

4. The **Pencil** tool should be active. Click and drag across the window to make a drawing.

Close Button

5. Click the **Close** button, ▐X▌. As the application is processing a drawing, there will be a warning message. Click **Don't Save**. The window will close.

6. Click **Start** and select **Computer** from the **Start** menu.

7. As an alternative method of closing a window, right click on the **Title Bar** and select **Close** from the shortcut menu.

ℹ️ *The window can also be closed by right clicking its button on the **Taskbar** and selecting **Close window** or by pressing <Alt F4>.*

Driving Lesson 10 - Scroll Bars

 Park and Read

When a window in any application is too small to display all the information in it, the window automatically adds **scroll bars**. Scroll bars are added horizontally and/or vertically, depending on the hidden information.

Scroll bars are used in many other places where there is hidden data, for example, in drop down lists.

Manoeuvres

1. If there is no icon on the **Desktop** for **Control Panel**, click **Start**, right click on **Control Panel**, then click **Show on Desktop**.

2. Click a blank area of the **Desktop** to remove the **Start** menu.

3. Double click the **Control Panel** icon on the **Desktop**. Make sure the window is <u>not</u> maximised, click the **Restore Down** button, 🗗 , if necessary.

4. Reduce the size of the window to show only 4 icons. The vertical **Scroll Bar** is displayed. This means that there is not enough space in the current window to show all the content of this display (all of the icons).

Vertical Scroll Bar

continued over

Driving Lesson 10 - Continued

5. The vertical scroll bar can be used to scroll up and down in the window. A scroll bar consists of scroll arrows at either end of the bar and a scroll button.

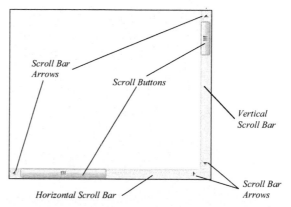

Scroll Bar Arrows

Scroll Buttons

Vertical Scroll Bar

Horizontal Scroll Bar

Scroll Bar Arrows

6. The position of the button indicates the relative position of the current view and the size of the button indicates how much of the available information is being displayed. Look at the previous picture of the **Control Panel** window. The scroll button is at the top of the bar, so the top part of the data is being displayed. The button is about half the size of the bar, so about half of the available data is being displayed.

> **i** *The scroll buttons reduce in size as the window becomes smaller, i.e. less of the available information is shown.*

7. The scroll button can be moved by means of the arrows or by dragging. Click on the down arrow of the right vertical scroll bar to move the area displayed in the window down gradually. Continue to do this until the scroll button is at the bottom of the scroll bar.

8. Click and drag the vertical scroll button to the top of the bar.

> **i** *To move the display of a window up/down more quickly, click once on the vertical scroll bar between the scroll button and the top/bottom arrow.*

9. Close the **Control Panel** window.

Driving Lesson 11 - System Properties

▣ Park and Read

System Properties can be viewed to show information relating to the computer.

☞ Manoeuvres

1. Display the **Start** menu and right click on **Computer**.

2. Select **Properties** from the shortcut menu.

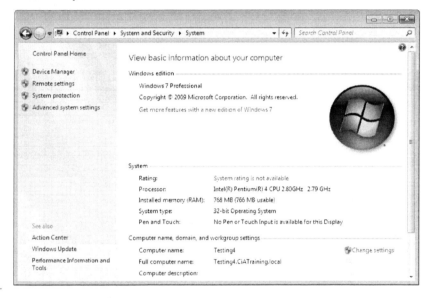

3. Read the information. The current *Windows* edition information is displayed, and the type of processor and the amount of memory are displayed under **System**. The computer name and network details are also shown.

4. Click **Device Manager** from the panel on the left of the window to see information on the hardware devices which make up your computer.

ℹ️ *Depending on how security has been set up on your computer, there may be a **User Account Control** message displayed asking permission to continue. Click the **Continue** button in the message box. These messages may appear at other times during the exercises in this guide.*

continued over

Driving Lesson 11 - Continued

5.   A list of all attached device types will appear (it may be different to that shown above).

6.   Click on the ▷ symbol next to a device type. The exact make and model of any device(s) of this type which are present will be listed. To see more information on some of the devices, right click on the device name and then select **Properties** from the shortcut menu.

7.   Do not change any of the properties. Click **Cancel** to close the **Properties** dialog box.

8.   Use the **Close** button to close the **Device Manager** window and return to the **System** window.

9.   Click on **Advanced system settings**. A **System Properties** dialog box is displayed where changes can be made with regard to **Performance, User Profiles** and **Startup and Recovery** settings.

10.   Click the **Settings** button under each heading to view the settings, clicking **Cancel** in each dialog box to return to **System Properties**.

11.   Click the **Cancel** button to close the **System Properties** dialog box.

12.   Use the **Close** button to close the **System** window and return to the **Desktop**.

Driving Lesson 12 - Using Help

⯀P Park and Read

Windows has a built in **Help** facility to assist the user when information is required.

⟫ Manoeuvres

1.   Select the **Start** button and then select **Help and Support**. Several forms of helpful information are available from this window.

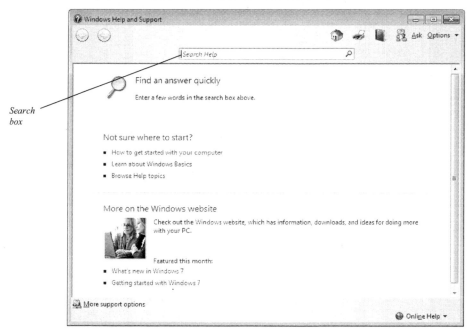

Search box

2.   Click on **Learn about Windows Basics**. This displays a list of articles covering basic topics about your computer and *Windows 7*.

3.   Click the text **Using your mouse**. A detailed article about the computer mouse is displayed.

4.   To obtain a printed copy of this information, click the **Print** button, ⊠.

5.   Click the **Back** button, ⊚, to return to the previous screen. Click the **Back** button again to return to the **Help and Support** home window.

continued over

Driving Lesson 12 - Continued

6. Click the **Browse Help** icon, . This displays general help for *Windows* arranged like chapters in a book.

7. Click the text **Printers and printing**.

8. This displays a list of help topic headings which can be expanded. Click **Install a printer** to expand the heading and see the help text.

9. Click the **Home** button, to return to the **Help and Support** window.

10. A quick method of locating help is to use the **Search** box at the top of the window. Type **paint** in the box and click the **Search Help** button, .

11. A list of topics matching the search is displayed. Click the text **Using Paint** to display help about the **Paint** application.

12. Click **Home** to return and clear the **Search** box by selecting the text and pressing the **Delete** button. Type **desktop background** in the **Search** box and click the **Search Help** button.

13. A list of matching topics is displayed. Some of these may match desktop or background but the best results (matching both words) will be shown first. Click the text **Change your desktop background (wallpaper)**, read the help text then click **Home,** , to return.

14. Click the **Online Help** button in the bottom right corner of the window and make sure that **Get online Help** is active.

15. Click **What's new in Windows 7**. This is a link to a *Microsoft* help website (requires an active Internet connection). This article highlights some of the new features of *Windows 7*.

16. Use the **Close** button, to close the browser window and return to the **Help and Support** window.

*Some system windows and dialog boxes can access relevant areas of the help system directly by means of a **Help** menu or **Help** button* .

*Most applications have their own internal **Help** systems with content that is relevant to their operation. Application **Help** will be described in the appropriate application guides.*

17. Close the **Help and Support** window by clicking its **Close** button, .

Driving Lesson 13 - Shut Down and Restart

▣ Park and Read

If a computer is shut down abnormally, e.g. switched off in mid task, any unsaved data in an application can be lost and storage space within the computer can be corrupted. Shutting down properly prevents this and ensures that programs are closed and all data is saved correctly.

Normally, you should never need to reset the computer, while switched on. Sometimes, however, there may be problems and the computer could lock up, which means that it does not respond to moving the mouse or any key presses. The only course of action in this circumstance is to reset the computer.

↱ Manoeuvres

1. To close *Windows*, make sure all applications are closed, and click **Start**. Look at the buttons at the bottom of the right panel.

2. The **Shut Down** button when clicked closes down the computer. Click the arrow at the right of the bar, [▷], to see the other close down options.

Switch User	Changes users without closing programs.
Log Off	Closes all programs and logs off current user.
Lock	Locks the user session.
Restart	Close all programs, close *Windows*, then start *Windows* again.
Sleep	Saves the session then puts the computer in a low power state.
Hibernate	Saves the session to the hard disk then turns off the computer.

ℹ *Some of these options may be missing or unavailable (greyed out) depending on the configuration of your computer.*

3. Click the **Restart** option. *Windows* is shut down and then immediately starts up again without the power being switched off. This process is often used after installing new hardware or software in order for it to be detected by the operating system.

4. Display the **Start** menu. If the **Sleep** option is available on the shut down options, click on it. All open documents and programs are saved to memory and the computer will be shut down to standby power.

continued over

Driving Lesson 13 - Continued

5. Log on and then display the **Start** menu. If the **Sleep** option is available on the shut down options, click on it. All open documents and programs are saved to memory and the computer will be shut down to standby power.

6. To wake the computer from sleep, press any key or click the mouse. If this does not work try pressing the computer **Power** button. The computer will quickly waken and prompt you to sign in again. It will then resume operation exactly where it was previously.

7. Display the **Start** menu. If the **Hibernate** option is available on the shut down options, click on it. All open documents and programs are saved to the disk, the power is switched off and the computer will be completely shut down. There may be a short delay before the power is turned off.

i *When the computer is shut down as the result of a command, it will either display a message instructing you to switch off the power, or switch off the power automatically as part of the process. If the monitor light remains on, switch the monitor off too. The computer is now switched off completely.*

8. To wake the computer from hibernation, press the computer **Power** button. The computer will start, prompt you to sign in again and resume operation from exactly where it was previously.

9. Click the **Shut Down** button from the **Start** menu. All open programs are closed, it is your responsibility to save any unsaved work. The computer will then completely shut down.

10. To start the computer after a **Shut Down**, press the computer **Power** button. The computer will start with *Windows* running but no other applications will be active.

i *Follow one of these actions (**Sleep**, **Hibernate**, or **Shut Down**) every time you wish to turn off the computer. NEVER switch the power off when the **Desktop** is displayed, ALWAYS close down properly from the **Start Menu**.*

11. Look at the front panel of your computer and locate the **Reset** button. Often this button is not labelled and you might have to refer to the documentation supplied with your computer to identify it. Pressing this button will shut down the computer immediately without saving any work and then start it up again. The only time this button should be used is to recover from a situation when neither the keyboard nor the mouse is responding.

Driving Lesson 14 - Revision

This Driving Lesson covers the features introduced in this section. Try not to refer to the previous Driving Lessons while completing it.

1. Begin this Driving Lesson with the computer switched off. Start the computer.

2. There should be a **Recycle Bin** icon on your **Desktop**. What action is necessary to activate this and display the contents?

3. Display the contents of the **Recycle Bin**. Are they displayed in;

    a) a window

    b) a dialog box

    c) a shortcut menu

    Close the **Recycle Bin**.

4. **Auto Arrange** the **Desktop** icons.

5. Arrange the **Desktop** icons by **Item**.

6. Turn off **Auto Arrange**.

7. Display the **Control Panel** window.

8. Reduce the size of the window and move it to the top right corner of the screen.

9. **Maximise** the window, then **Restore** it.

10. Close the window.

11. Use **Help** to find out about **Starting a Program by using the Run command**. Read the **Help** window.

12. Close the **Help** window.

13. Shut down the computer.

---

[i] *Answers to this revision exercise can be found at the end of this guide.*

If you experienced any difficulty completing this Revision, refer back to the Driving Lessons in this section. Then redo the Revision.

Once you are confident with the features, complete the Record of Achievement Matrix referring to the section, at the end of the guide. Only when competent move on to the next Section.

Section 2
Managing Files

By the end of this Section you should be able to:

Understand Drives, Files and Folders

Understand File Types

Backup to a Removable Storage Device

Copy, Move, Rename and Delete Files/Folders

Create Folders

Use the Recycle Bin

Search for Files/Folders

To gain an understanding of the above features, work through the **Driving Lessons** in this **Section**.

For each **Driving Lesson**, read the **Park and Read** instructions, without touching the keyboard, then work through the numbered steps of the **Manoeuvres** on the computer. Complete the **Revision Exercise(s)** at the end of the section to test your knowledge.

Driving Lesson 15 - File Storage

◤ Park and Read

Computer systems store their data and programs on a variety of **Storage Devices**. The type and number of these devices can vary from one computer to another, but the operating system will always display the contents of these devices in a number of useful ways.

The vast majority of computers have a **Hard Disk Drive** (HDD) which is the main storage device for the system. These can store many Gigabytes of data, which can be accessed very quickly (access times measured in milliseconds). Traditionally this is referred to as drive **C**. It is possible however to have further such drives installed, which would then become drive **D**, etc.

Hard Disk Drives that are part of the computer are known as **Local Drives**, but if the computer is part of a network it may be possible to access drives on other connected computers. These drives are then known as **Network Drives**.

Computers usually have a few **USB** ports. These are used to connect various devices to the computer. USB **flash memory** sticks can be attached in this way and used as a form of storage.

Often, when computers are networked, there will be an area for data storage on another machine, i.e. you may save your data to a drive on a remote computer, rather than to a drive on your own computer. This is called a **network drive**.

Online file storage is a facility that is becoming more popular. It allows you to save files to a specific hard drive on the Internet. There are many web sites that provide free online storage. With this convenient service, you can access your own files and share files via any PC with Internet access.

A **Compact Disk Drive** uses compact disks as the storage media, each compact disk holding at present about 700 Mb. Some drives will only read from existing CDs, others (CD writers) allow data to be written onto a blank **CD**; this is a **CD-RW** drive (Read Write). Most computers now have a **DVD** or **DVD-RW** drive; they are almost identical in principle to **CD** drives, but can hold several Gigabytes of data. **CD/DVD** devices are assigned drive letters after the last hard disk drive.

◠ Manoeuvres

1. Start up the computer and click the **Start** button. Click on the **Computer** option to display the storage devices available on your computer.

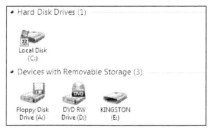

continued over

Driving Lesson 15 - Continued

2. This is the configuration of a typical system with a local hard disk (**drive C:**), a **Floppy Disk Drive (A:**), **DVD RW Drive (D:**) and a memory stick in a USB port, **UDISK (E:**). The content of the display will be different on your computer. There are several formats in which to view this data and your display may not look like that above. Click the drop down arrow on the **Change your view** button, [image] to see the options.

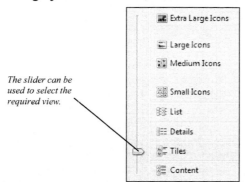

The slider can be used to select the required view.

3. The view options are varied and are used in different circumstances or by personal preference. Select each view in turn using the **Change your view** button. The same data is shown in a different format.

4. Select the **Details** view, this shows size and free space.

Name	Type	Total Size	Free Space
◢ Hard Disk Drives (1)			
💾 Local Disk (C:)	Local Disk	37.2 GB	26.0 GB
◢ Devices with Removable Storage (3)			
💾 Floppy Disk Drive (A:)	Floppy Disk Drive		
💿 DVD RW Drive (D:)	CD Drive		
🔌 UDISK (E:)	Removable Disk	3.72 GB	2.54 GB

5. Double click **Disk (C:)** to display the contents of the drive. Make sure **Details** view is still selected to see details of the contents.

Name	Date modified	Type	Size
📁 PerfLogs	14/07/2009 03:37	File folder	
📁 Program Files	22/12/2009 10:30	File folder	
📁 Users	14/12/2009 13:28	File folder	
📁 Windows	11/12/2009 11:49	File folder	

continued over

Driving Lesson 15 - Continued

i   *The **Size** column only applies when files are included in the list.*

6.   Click the **Back** button, 🔙, to return to the previous screen then select the **Large Icons** view.

7.   The two figures on a **Local Disk** icon indicate that the device is being shared and its contents may be accessed by other computers on the network. This may not apply on your system.

8.   Right click on the **Local Disk** icon and select **Properties** from the shortcut menu. A dialog box showing detailed properties of the disk is displayed, including the total capacity of the device and the remaining free space.

Local Disk (C:) Properties		✖

Security	Previous Versions	Quota
General	Tools	Hardware	Sharing

Type: Local Disk
File system: NTFS

■   Used space: 11,135,451,136 bytes   10.3 GB
■   Free space: 148,798,599,168 bytes   138 GB

Capacity: 159,934,050,304 bytes   148 GB

Drive C: [Disk Cleanup]

☐ Compress this drive to save disk space
☑ Allow files on this drive to have contents indexed in addition to file properties

[OK]   [Cancel]   [Apply]

9.   Look at the information available then click **OK** to close the **Properties** dialog box.

10.   The contents of any device can be displayed by double clicking the icon. Double click **Local Disk (C:)** to see the contents of the hard disk.

11.   Close the display by clicking the **Close** button, ✖.

Driving Lesson 16 - Folders and Files

▣ Park and Read

In order to assist in storing and finding files and programs on the hard disk, *Windows* uses **Folders**. Any storage device, hard disk, floppy disk, memory stick or CD/DVD, can be split into many folders, each containing all the files related to a specific task or program. A folder may also contain other folders, thus sub-dividing the disk even further. The concept is much like organising a filing cabinet by having separate drawers and files for each particular task.

A folder in *Windows 7* appears as an icon, with the name of the folder printed next to or underneath it depending on the view displayed. Different folders may show different internal detail. When an icon is double clicked, the folder opens and its contents are displayed.

Windows 7 has a new feature called a **Library**. A **Library** gathers information from different locations and displays them as a single collection, without moving them from where they are stored. When new to file management this concept is difficult to grasp.

↟ Manoeuvres

1. Select **Start** then **Documents**. This will run **Windows Explorer** and display the contents of the **Documents** library.

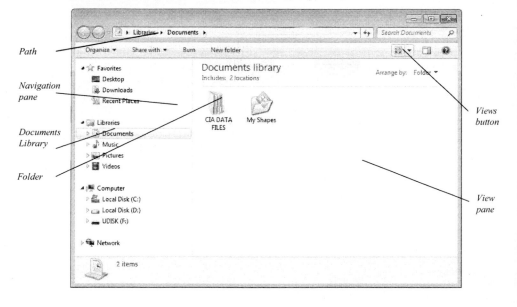

Path

Navigation pane

Documents Library

Folder

Views button

View pane

continued over

Driving Lesson 16 - Continued

i   *The contents of your **Documents** library may be different to that above. There are also different views of the same information.*

2.   Click the drop down arrow on the **Views** button, [icon] and make sure the slider is positioned next to **Tiles**. Views are covered in the next exercise.

3.   If the data files which accompany this guide have been installed correctly there will be a folder **CIA DATA FILES** within the **My Documents** folder in the **Documents** library. Double click the **CIA DATA FILES** folder icon in the **View** pane to display its contents. There will be a folder **ECDL** in the contents. Double click that to display its contents.

> Documents library
> ECDL   Arrange by: Folder ▾
>
>   📁 2 Managing Files   📁 3 Word Processing
>   File folder   File folder
>
>   📁 4 Spreadsheets   📁 5 Databases
>   File folder   File folder
>
>   📁 6 Presentations
>   File folder

4.   Double click **2 Managing Files** to open the folder and display the files contained in it. Click the **Views** button drop down arrow then select **Details** to see the files listed in a condensed view with more information.

5.   If file extensions, e.g. **.txt,** are not displayed with the file names, click
     [Organize ▾], select **Folder and search options** and click on the **View** tab. Make sure that the **Hide extensions for known file types** is unchecked. Click **OK**. The file extensions will be displayed.

i   *Files types are identified by extensions, e.g. **.docx** for a Word document.*

6.   Click **Documents** under **Libraries** in the **Navigation pane** on the left.

7.   The **Documents library** is arranged by **Folder** by default. Locate the **Arrange by** field in the **View** pane and click the down triangle to the right of **Folder** to see the various options.

8.   Select **Name**. This now shows all the files within the **Library** from all the various folders, in alphabetic order. This view enables a file to be easily found if you cannot remember where it was stored.

9.   Close the window using the **Close** button, [X].

10. Open the **Documents** window again. The display still shows **Arrange by: Name**. Drop down the list and select **Folder**, the default display.

11. Close the window using the **Close** button, [X].

Driving Lesson 17 - Navigation

Park and Read

The program which displays the organisation of drives, files and folders in the computer is called *Windows Explorer*. This is the program that runs when **Computer** or **Documents** is selected from the **Start** menu.

It displays the storage of data on a computer in a hierarchical way; that is, it will show the main devices or libraries available to the computer, each device or library can then be expanded to show the component folders and files, and each folder can be further expanded down to the lowest possible level. Folder structure is shown in the **Navigation pane** on the left, contents are shown in the **View pane** on the right.

Different views are available in the **View pane**, including a **Details** view which can show many properties of the folder contents. File sizes are measured in **KB**, **MB** and **GB**.

1GB = 1,000 MB, 1MB = 1,000 KB.

The size of a spreadsheet file may be 20KB, a high quality image file perhaps 600KB, a folder containing many of these images possibly several MB. A folder containing a large collection of digital photos or a modern action game may be several GB.

The program can also be used to control the copying, moving, creating and deleting of files and folders, known as **File Management**.

Manoeuvres

1. Select **Start** and click on **Documents** to open that window. Set the **View** to **Tiles**

2. Another way to navigate through the folders on your computer is to use the **Navigation pane** on the left. Move the cursor to this area and notice that the **Documents** library has an ▷ icon in front of it. This means that the folder has subfolders.

3. Click once on ▷ next to **Documents**. The subfolders are displayed underneath the main folder and the icon changes to a ◢ icon. This is called *expanding* a folder.

4. To hide the subfolders, click the ◢ icon next to **Documents**. The ◢ icon changes to a ▷ icon again and the subfolders or files are hidden. This is called *collapsing* a folder. When a folder has no ▷ icon, there are no further folders within it and it cannot be expanded.

5. Expand the **Documents** library again in the **Navigation pane**.

6. Expand **My Documents** folder, then the **CIA DATA FILES** folder.

continued over

Driving Lesson 17 - Continued

7. Expand the **ECDL** folder, this contains all the data files required to study for this qualification.

    > ECDL
    >   2 Managing Files
    >   3 Word Processing
    >   4 Spreadsheets
    >   5 Databases
    >   6 Presentations

8. Click once on the **2 Managing Files** folder to display the files in it. The contents of the folder are shown in the **View pane**.

9. Click the drop down arrow on the **Views** button, and select **Details**. The folder contents now have their name, size, type and date modified shown. This enables the smallest, largest, newest, oldest and files of the same type to be identified.

File Icons

Name	Date modified	Type	Size
Advert.docx	20/02/2007 11:16	Microsoft Office ...	11 KB
Banking.docx	21/02/2007 14:21	Microsoft Office ...	11 KB
Bowler.jpg	05/10/1999 08:34	JPEG image	71 KB
Budget.xlsx	20/02/2007 11:19	Microsoft Office E...	10 KB
Cam.docx	20/02/2007 11:17	Microsoft Office ...	11 KB
CIA Training Ltd - Overview.docx	20/02/2007 11:18	Microsoft Office ...	11 KB
Cia.docx	20/02/2007 12:17	Microsoft Office ...	11 KB
Clothing.docx	20/02/2007 11:18	Microsoft Office ...	11 KB
Contents.docx	20/02/2007 11:19	Microsoft Office ...	11 KB
Mailing.accdb	20/02/2007 11:31	Microsoft Office A...	288 KB
Marketing.pptx	20/02/2007 11:25	Microsoft Office P...	79 KB
micky&andrew video.avi	12/12/1999 02:11	Video Clip	115 KB
Notepad file.txt	05/12/1995 17:20	Text Document	1 KB
Photograph.tif	17/02/1993 10:24	TIFF image	48 KB
product.zip	24/09/2002 10:19	Compressed (zipp...	4 KB
test sound file.wav	31/01/1999 11:02	Wave Sound	19 KB
training sound file.wav	31/01/1999 11:02	Wave Sound	16 KB

10. Different types of files are displayed with a different icon before the name and the size, type and date when saved (modified) are all displayed. The number of files in the folder is displayed at the bottom of the window.

11. Use the **Views** button to display other possible views of the contents but leave it finally in **Details** view.

12. Leave the display open for the next exercise.

Driving Lesson 18 - File Types

P Park and Read

File types are represented by a 3 - 5 character file extension after a file name and tell the computer system what type of file it is. When a file is created by an application, e.g. spreadsheet, the correct file extension is automatically added. You can identify what type of file it is by the extension and by the icon displayed with the file.

Care should be taken when copying or renaming files to maintain the correct file extension. Changing the file extension does not change the file contents but will confuse the computer operating system. For example, if a spreadsheet file is given a **.docx** extension and then double clicked, *Word* will attempt to open it and there will be an error.

Some common file types are listed here:

.docx	*Word 2007* document.
.accdb	*Access 2007* database.
.pptx	*PowerPoint 2007* presentation.
.xlsx	*Excel 2007* spreadsheet.
.avi, **.mpeg**	Video files.
.exe	Executable file, i.e. a program.
.jpg, **.tif**, **.gif**	Image files.
.tmp	Temporary file. One used by the system during a process and then deleted automatically.
.txt, **.rtf**	Generic text files.
.pdf	Portable document format files.
.wav, **.mp3**	Audio or Sound files.
.zip	A compressed (zipped) archive file. These are described in a later Section.

Manoeuvres

1.   From the display of files in the **2 Managing Files** folder, identify each of the file types in the folder just by the icon and the file extension.

i *Remember, if file extensions are not displayed with the file names, click* [Organize ▼]*, select **Folder and search options** and click on the **View** tab. Make sure that the **Hide extensions for known file types** is unchecked. Click **OK** to display the file extensions.*

2.   Display the contents of each of the other subfolders of **ECDL** in turn and identify all of the file types found there.

Driving Lesson 19 - Sorting File Displays

▣ Park and Read

The list of files shown in the **View pane** of any window can be presented in different ways. As well as the different **View** options covered already, the files can be shown in different orders, i.e. sorted.

↪ Manoeuvres

1. Use the **Navigation pane** to display a list of the files in the **2 Managing Files** folder. Make sure **Details** view is selected. Adjust the column widths if necessary to display all data as below. To adjust the columns, click and drag the borders between columns on the **Header bar**.

Header bar ——

Name	Date modified	Type	Size
Advert.docx	20/02/2007 12:16	Microsoft Office Word Document	11 KB
Banking.docx	21/02/2007 15:21	Microsoft Office Word Document	11 KB
Bowler.jpg	05/10/1999 09:34	JPEG image	71 KB
Budget.xlsx	20/02/2007 12:19	Microsoft Office Excel Worksheet	10 KB
Cam.docx	20/02/2007 12:17	Microsoft Office Word Document	11 KB
CIA Training Ltd - Overview.docx	20/02/2007 12:18	Microsoft Office Word Document	11 KB
Cia.docx	20/02/2007 13:17	Microsoft Office Word Document	11 KB
Clothing.docx	20/02/2007 12:18	Microsoft Office Word Document	11 KB
Contents.docx	20/02/2007 12:19	Microsoft Office Word Document	11 KB
Mailing.accdb	20/02/2007 12:31	Microsoft Office Access 2007 Database	288 KB
Marketing.pptx	20/02/2007 12:25	Microsoft Office PowerPoint Presentation	79 KB
micky&andrew video.avi	12/12/1999 03:11	Video Clip	115 KB
Notepad file.txt	05/12/1995 18:20	Text Document	1 KB
Photograph.tif	17/02/1993 11:24	TIFF image	48 KB
product.zip	24/09/2002 11:19	Compressed (zipped) Folder	4 KB
test sound file.wav	31/01/1999 12:02	Wave Sound	19 KB
training sound file.wav	31/01/1999 12:02	Wave Sound	16 KB

2. The default sequence for the display is alphabetical by name. This is useful if you need to find a specifically named file. Click the **Name** column heading ⌊Name⌋ to change to reverse alphabetic order.

3. Click the **Size** column heading to sort the list in order of size, largest first (descending). This is useful to find the largest files in a folder. Click the heading again to display in the reverse order (ascending).

4. Click the **Type** column heading to sort the display by **File type**. This will group all similar files and is useful if you want to see and count all the files of one type, e.g. all the *Word* documents.

5. Click the **Date modified** column heading to change the display order to the date the file was last changed, most recent first. This is useful to find the files in a folder that have been most recently used. Click it again to display in reverse order.

6. Click the **Name** heading again to sort then file names back into alphabetical order, then close the window.

Driving Lesson 20 - Creating New Folders

▣ Park and Read

New folders are created to organise files and keep files relating to a similar subject together. There is a **New Folder** button which can be used to create a new folder. Alternatively, you can right click in the **View pane** of a folder and use the shortcut menu. A folder within another is called a **subfolder**. When creating new folders (and files), take care to use meaningful names, to be able to organise and identify them later.

⌒ Manoeuvres

1. Display the **Start** menu and open the **Documents** window.

2. Expand **CIA DATA FILES** then **ECDL**. Click on the **2 Managing Files** folder to display its contents.

3. Click the **New folder** button, New folder , on the toolbar. A new folder will appear with its name highlighted in blue, ready for the new name to be entered, New folder .

4. Type in the name **Reports**. Press <**Enter**> to complete the process. The folder is created and named.

5. There is another way to create folders. Right click in a blank area of the **View pane** of **2 Managing Files**. From the shortcut menu select **New** then **Folder** and name the new folder **Media**. Press <**Enter**>.

6. Folders within other folders are called **subfolders**. The folder **2 Managing Files** now has two new subfolders, **Reports** and **Media**, as well as the **product** compressed folder.

7. Now select the **My Documents** folder in the **Navigation pane**.

8. Create a **New Folder**, enter your first name as the folder name and press <**Enter**>.

9. Click on this new folder in the **Navigation pane** to display its contents. It is empty. Create a subfolder within it and call the subfolder **Sample**. Move the mouse pointer into the **Navigation pane** and your folder now has a ▷ next to it.

10. Expand your folder to see the **Sample** subfolder listed. Click the **Sample** folder to open it. It is empty.

11. Every open window has an **Address bar** that displays your current location. Clicking on a location in the **Address bar** navigates directly to it. Click on **My Documents** to display its contents.

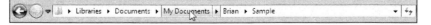

Driving Lesson 21 - Copying Files and Folders

▣ Park and Read

To work with a file, click on it once in the **View pane**, this highlights the file showing that it is selected.

> 🖼 Bowler.jpg
> 📊 Budget.xlsx
> 📄 Cam.docx

Selected files can be copied in a variety of ways: by dragging from one location to another using the left or right mouse button or by using the menu commands.

Copying important files from the hard disk to a different drive, usually a CD or DVD, is known as creating a backup. These backup copies are an insurance against the original data ever being lost or corrupted, due to virus action, accidental deletion or catastrophic hard disk failure, for example. Backups should be made regularly and stored off site.

⌒ Manoeuvres

1. Make sure a newly formatted floppy or a blank disk is in the **A:** drive or an external storage device is attached to receive the copies. Make sure the **My Documents** window is displayed.

2. Locate the **Computer** icon (you may need to scroll down the **Navigation pane** to find it) and expand it to see the external storage device icon.

3. Expand **CIA DATA FILES** then **ECDL**. Click on the **2 Managing Files** folder to display its contents.

4. Click and drag the file **Advert** across to the floppy disk icon or other storage device in the **Navigation pane**. When the cursor is over the destination, a tooltip message is displayed confirming that the file is being *copied*.

continued over

Driving Lesson 23 - Selecting Multiple Files

Park and Read

Often in file management, more than one file at a time needs to be copied, moved or deleted. This means that multiple files need to be selected; there are various ways of doing this.

Manoeuvres

1. Display the contents of the **2 Managing Files** folder.

2. View the contents as a list, by clicking the **Views** button then selecting **List** from the menu.

3. To select a range of files, click once on the file, **Budget**, hold down the **<Shift>** key on the keyboard, then click on the file, **Mailing**. Release the **<Shift>** key. All the files in between will be selected. The number of files will be shown at the bottom of the window.

4. Click in the **View pane** away from the selection to deselect all files.

5. To select multiple files that are not in a range, hold down <Ctrl> on the keyboard and click on all the files to be selected. Use <Ctrl> to select files as in the following diagram.

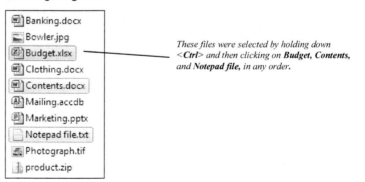

These files were selected by holding down *<Ctrl> and then clicking on **Budget, Contents,** and **Notepad file,** in any order.*

continued over

Driving Lesson 23 - Continued

6.   Click in the **View pane** away from the files to cancel the selection.

i *All methods of selecting multiple objects work equally well in any of the **Change your view** options.*

7.   To select all the files and folders currently in the **View** window, click the **Organize** button then select **Select all** from the menu.

8.   Click in the **View pane** away from the files to cancel the selection.

9.   Alternatively, press **<Ctrl A>** to select all the files currently in the **View** window.

10.   Once multiple files have been selected, many of the processes that can be applied to a single file such as drag and drop or copy and paste can be applied to the group of selected files. With all the content of the **2 Managing Files** folder selected, click the **Organize** button then select **Copy**.

11.   Locate and select the **Sample** folder that was moved into the **ECDL** folder in the previous Driving Lesson.

12.   Click the **Organize** button then select **Paste**. All the selected files and folders are copied to the **Sample** folder.

i *All the instructions in this Driving Lesson and the two previous lessons, which refer to files, apply to all objects (files and folders) in <u>exactly</u> the same way folders and files can be selected, copied and moved in an identical manner. Mixtures of files and folders can be selected, copied or moved in the same operation.*

Driving Lesson 24 - Viewing Object Properties

▣ Park and Read

To view the properties of any object (folder or file), right click on it and select **Properties**. A properties dialog box appears giving information about the **Type**, **Location**, **Size**, when **Created**, **Modified** and the **Attributes** of the object.

⌒ Manoeuvres

1.   To view the properties of an object, point and right click on it. Right click on the folder **2 Managing Files**.

2.   From the shortcut menu click **Properties** to display the **Properties** dialog box.

> **2 Managing Files Properties**   ✕
>
> | General | Sharing | Security | Previous Versions |
>
> 2 Managing Files
>
> Type: File folder
> Location: C:\Users\Ian Chapman\Documents\CIA DATA FILE
> Size: 720 KB (738,171 bytes)
> Size on disk: 744 KB (761,856 bytes)
> Contains: 17 Files, 2 Folders
>
> Created: 20 October 2009, 09:20:41
>
> Attributes: ■ Read-only (Only applies to files in folder)
>   ☐ Hidden   Advanced...
>
>   OK   Cancel   Apply

3.   Note that the **Contains** value shows the total number of files and other folders within this folder, even if some of those objects are in subfolders.

continued over

Driving Lesson 24 - Continued

4.   If the **Read-only** attribute for an object file is set, that object can be opened and read but cannot be amended under its own name; the file is locked. To allow a file to be amended (Read/Write access), this attribute must be unchecked.

i *If the **Read-only** attribute for a folder is set or cleared, there is an option to apply the change to all files and subfolders.*

5.   Click on the **Cancel** button to close the dialog box.

6.   Right click on the **Banking.docx** file in the **2 Managing Files** folder, and select **Properties**. The **General** page of the dialog box shows information as before.

7.   Select the **Details** tab in the dialog box to see detailed information on the file content. Scroll up and down to see all the information, including statistical data, e.g. number of pages and word count.

Banking.docx Properties

General | Security | Details | Previous Versions

Property	Value
Last saved by	Brian
Revision number	3
Version number	
Program name	Microsoft Office Word
Company	CIA Training Ltd
Manager	
Content created	20/02/2007 11:16
Date last saved	21/02/2007 14:21
Last printed	
Total editing time	00:01:00
Content	
Status	
Content type	
Pages	1
Word count	121
Character count	696
Line count	5
Paragraph count	1

Remove Properties and Personal Information

OK | Cancel | Apply

---

8.   Click **Cancel** to close the dialog box.

9.   Examine the **Properties** of some of the other files in the folder, closing the **Properties** dialog boxes after opening.

Driving Lesson 25 - Renaming Files and Folders

▣ Park and Read

Files and **Folders** can be renamed to help with their management. Care should be taken not to change file extensions when renaming, as file extensions determine which application is used when a file is opened.

Some care should be given to the names assigned to new files and folders. When there are hundreds of files and folders stored on your disk it may be difficult to exactly locate the required item. This will be more difficult if the assigned names have no structure, such as **New folder**, or **Document26**.

Try and assign names that mean something such as **Budget 2010** and **Office Relocation** for folders; or **Projected Expenses 2010** and **New Office Floor Plan** for files. Rather than store hundreds of mixed files in a single folder, use a logical structured hierarchy of folders which will help to organise your files and make them easier to manage.

☞ Manoeuvres

1. In the **My Documents** folder locate the folder **2 Managing Files** and display its contents in the **View pane**.

2. Display the contents of the **Media** folder, then right click on **micky&andrew video** to display a shortcut menu.

3. Select the **Rename** option from the menu.

4. The name **micky&andrew video** is now highlighted. Type in **video file** and press **<Enter>**. The file name is changed.

i *Even if the file extension **.avi** is displayed, it is not automatically included in the rename process. Trying to change a file extension will result in a warning message.*

i *If the user clicks on a file in the **View pane**, waits for a second, and clicks again, the name can be highlighted for renaming. This happens accidentally sometimes when a double click is performed too slowly.*

5. Folder names can be changed in a similar way by selecting the folder, right clicking and selecting **Rename**. Use this method to change the **Media** folder name to **Video Clips**.

Driving Lesson 26 - Deleting Files and Folders

▣ Park and Read

Files and folders can be deleted in four main ways:

a. Select the object by clicking on it, then press the **<Delete>** key.

b. Right click on the file/folder and select **Delete** from the menu.

c. Click and drag the file/folder over the **Recycle Bin** icon on the **Desktop** then release the icon "into" the bin (the Recycle Bin is covered in the next Driving Lesson).

d. Select the file/folder and select **Delete** from the **Organize** button menu.

ℹ️ *The result of deleting a file depends on its location. If the file is deleted from the hard disk, the file is moved to the Recycle Bin. If the file is deleted from a floppy disk or portable storage device, then it is deleted permanently.*

☞ Manoeuvres

1. Open the **ECDL** folder and display the contents of the **Sample** folder.

2. In the **View pane**, locate the **Reports** folder, and click on it to select it. Press the **<Delete>** key.

3. A message appears, confirming that the folder and its contents are to be deleted. Select **Yes** and the folder will be removed to the **Recycle Bin**.

4. Right click on **Contents** in the **Sample** folder, then select **Delete** from the menu. At the message, select **No**, to keep the file.

5. Click and drag the **Contents** file from the **Sample** folder to the **Recycle Bin** icon on the **Desktop**, (if necessary reduce the size of the **Sample** folder window first so that the **Recycle Bin** can be seen). The file is deleted.

6. Select **Budget** from the **Sample** folder. Click **Organize** then **Delete** to delete the **Budget** file.

7. Click **Yes** in the **Delete File** box to confirm the deletion, then close the window.

Driving Lesson 27 - The Recycle Bin

▣ Park and Read

When files or folders are deleted, they are not instantly removed from the hard disk. They are held in the **Recycle Bin**, whose icon can be seen on the **Desktop**. All deleted items are stored there until the **Recycle Bin** is emptied. Until then, the files can be restored. Objects deleted from a floppy disk or other portable storage devices are **not** held in the **Recycle Bin**, but are deleted immediately.

⌐ Manoeuvres

1. The **Recycle Bin** icon is situated on the **Desktop** and the icon changes according to whether it contains any files, ▨ Recycle Bin, or is empty, ▨ Recycle Bin.

2. Double click on the **Recycle Bin** icon. The **Recycle Bin** window opens, showing a list of all items that have been deleted. Select **Details** view.

3. There may be many items listed if the **Recycle Bin** has not been emptied recently but the most recent items should be those deleted in the last exercise. In **Details** view, click the **Date Deleted** header to sort in descending date order if necessary.

Name	Original Location	Date Deleted	Size
Budget.xlsx	C:\Users\Trainer\...	16/02/2010 16:44	10 KB
Contents.docx	C:\Users\Trainer\...	16/02/2010 16:44	14 KB
Reports	C:\Users\Trainer\...	16/02/2010 16:44	28 KB

4. Click the **Budget** file to select it, then click Restore this item from the **toolbar**. The file is removed from the **Recycle Bin** and placed where it was before deletion.

ℹ️ *If the folder that contained the file has also been deleted, the **Recycle Bin** re-creates the folder in which to place the file.*

5. Restore the **Reports** folder in a similar manner then close the **Recycle Bin** window.

6. Right click on the **Recycle Bin** icon. From the shortcut menu, select **Empty Recycle Bin** (if there are no files in the **Recycle Bin**, this option is not available). A message is displayed.

7. To avoid losing everything from the **Recycle Bin** at this time, select **No**. Clicking **Yes** would permanently remove all contents of the **Recycle Bin**.

8. Open the **Documents** window from the **Start Menu**. Open the **ECDL** folder and delete the **Sample** folder, to send it to the **Recycle Bin**.

9. Close the **Documents** window.

Driving Lesson 28 - Copy a Floppy Disk

▣ Park and Read

Data can be stored on a floppy disk as described earlier as a security backup or as a transfer method. This lesson describes how to make a copy of a floppy disk. It is only relevant if your computer has a floppy disk drive.

↱ Manoeuvres

1.   Ensure that you have a floppy disk drive, a floppy disk containing some data and a blank floppy disk to copy to, otherwise read this exercise for information only.

2.   Open the **Computer** window from the **Start** menu. Check the contents of a floppy disk in drive **A** to make sure that it contains data files.

3.   **Right click** on the **(A:)** drive icon, then select **Copy Disk**.

4.   The **Copy Disk** dialog box appears.

5.   To start the operation, click on the **Start** button. A prompt to insert the source disk appears.

6.   Insert the floppy disk to copy, if not already in the drive and click **OK**. The contents of the floppy disk are now read and a prompt to insert the destination disk appears.

7.   **Remove** the source disk and **insert** the destination disk. Click **OK**.

8.   The contents of the source disk are now copied to the destination disk. An exact copy is created. Any original data on the destination disk is lost.

9.   Select **Close** when completed.

10. Close the **Computer** window and remove the floppy disk from the drive.

Driving Lesson 29 - Searching for Files/Folders

▣ Park and Read

Not too long after purchasing the computer the user will probably have a large number of files stored in a variety of folders. It can become difficult to remember where every file is stored (this is where a well designed folder system is essential). If you cannot find a file, *Windows* has the ability to search for a required file or folder based on several criteria.

Searching is done using **Search Boxes** which are shown on every **Folder** view. Searches will then act on the contents of the current folder and subfolders. There is a **Search Box** at the bottom of the **Start** menu which will search all defined locations.

Search Options can be used to narrow down the search. All files that match the set criteria will be listed with their locations. It is important to decide whether you want to base the search on names of files or on content, e.g. words in a document.

Windows 7 maintains an automatic index of some files which makes searching in those areas very much quicker. By default, *Windows* indexes files in your personal folders, e.g. **Documents** and **email**.

⌕ Manoeuvres

1. Display the **Start** menu and select **Documents**. The contents of the **Document Library** are displayed. Select **Details** view.

2. Click in the **Search Box** at the top right of the window.

⬒ ⬛ ✖
Search   🔎

3. Type the word **cheques** into the box, slowly. The default search process is to find files with the search text in the content. If the folder is indexed, the search is narrowed as more letters are entered. The final result will show the file **Banking.docx**.

Ⓦ Banking.docx	Date modified: 02/04/2008 10:41
Online Banking With online banking you can track your finances 24 hours a day and take decisions inst...	Size: 10.7 KB
	Authors: BRIAN WALDRAM
C:\Users\Trainer\My Documents\CIA DATA FILES\ECDL\3 Word Processing	

 *Other files may be shown depending on the current content of the **Documents library**.*

continued over

Driving Lesson 29 - Continued

4.   In the **Navigation pane**, locate and select the **2 Managing Files** folder. Searches will now only be within this folder and its subfolders.

5.   It is possible to search for file names instead of content, by using the **name:** keyword. To only search for file names containing the text video, type **name:video** into the search box.

Documents library   Arrange by: Top results ▼
Search Results in 2 Managing Files

   Video Clips   Date modified: 16/02/2010 16:57
   C:\Users\Trainer\My Documents\CIA DATA FILES\ECDL\2 Managing Files

   video file.avi   Date modified: 12/12/1999 02:11
   Length: 00:00:04   Size: 114 KB

Search again in:
   Documents   Libraries   Computer   Custom...   Internet

6.   To create a new search, click the cross in the search box to clear the existing search or highlight the text and overtype with a new search.

7.   In a similar way specific types of files can be found. Type **type:xlsx** into the search box.

   Budget.xlsx   Date modified: 20/02/2007 11:19
   6000 6400 7200 6200 5300 5200 5500 5000 4000 3500 3800   Size: 9.82 KB
   3000 61100 6 6 6 6 6 6 6 6 6 6 6 6 36000 38400 43200 372...   Authors: Brian
   C:\Users\Trainer\My Documents\CIA DATA FILES\ECDL\2 Managing Files

8.   Search criteria can be combined to form more complex searches. Type **name:c type:docx** into the search box to find all *Word* document names starting with **c**.

ⓘ   *Actually any name which has a word starting with **c** will be found. A document named **New Chart** for example would also be selected.*

9.   The same result can be obtained using wildcards. Use * to represent any number of missing characters. Enter **type:txt name:n*** into the search box to select all **text** files starting with **n**.

10. Close the **Documents** window and click the **Start** button. There is a search box at the bottom of the **Start** menu which searches all defined locations. Type in **system** to find programs with the word **system** in the name and files which have the word **system** in their content.

11. Type **cashpoint** into the search box. There should be at least one file with that content.

12. Practise searching for files using different combinations of criteria.

Driving Lesson 30 - Advanced Searching

▣ Park and Read

More advanced searches can be performed in *Windows*. It is possible to search for files of a certain size or type, or those which have been modified on or between specific dates.

🏱 Manoeuvres

1.   Open the **Documents** window, then locate and select the **ECDL** folder.

2.   Type **abc** into the search box to display the search results window. There may be no matching items.

3.   To replace **abc** with **picture** in the search box, click ⊠ to the right of **abc** to clear the search then type **picture**. All picture files and others with picture in the content found in **ECDL** are listed.

4.   Searches can be made based on file size. With **picture** still selected, click in **Search** box to display the search options.

picture		×
Add a search filter		
Authors: Type: Date modified: Size:		

5.   Click on **Size** under **Add a search filter** and select **Small (10 – 100 KB)**.

picture size:		×
Empty (0 KB)		
Tiny (0 - 10 KB)		
Small (10 - 100 KB)		
Medium (100 KB - 1 MB)		
Large.(1 - 16 MB)		
Huge (16 - 128 MB)		
Gigantic (>128 MB)		

6.   All picture files in **ECDL** between 10 and 100 KB are listed. Notice how the selection criteria is shown in the search box.

picture size:small	×

7.   Click in the **Search** box and delete the contents. Searches can be made based on **Date modified**. Click in the **Search** box and select **Date modified**.

continued over

Driving Lesson 30 - Continued

8. For an exact date, select a date on the date selector. Click on today's date.

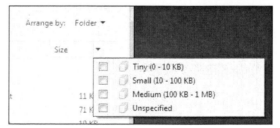

To select any date other than in the current month in the date selector use the left triangle to move through earlier months. Alternatively, click on the calendar heading to display months of the year. Click again to display a range of years. Click on the required year to select it, then a month, then a date.

9. All files in the **ECDL** folder which have been modified today are listed.

10. Complex searches can be created. Leave the **datemodified** selection, click in the search box and then click **Size** then select **Tiny (0 – 10 KB).**

11. All files modified today with a size up to 10KB are listed (note there may be none).

12. Searches can also be made by filtering individual folder listings. Click the folder **2 Managing Files** in the **Navigation pane**. This cancels the **Search** function.

13. Any one of the column headings in the **View pane** can be used to select files. Move the cursor over the **Size** column heading and click the arrow.

14. Check the **Tiny (0-10 KB)** box. Only files in this range are selected.

15. Click the arrows on the other column headings to see what selection options are available. Complex selection can be built up by applying a selection to more than one column.

16. A column with a selection applied is indicated by a tick, e.g. [Size ✓]. Click on **2 Managing Files** in the **Navigation pane** again to redisplay the contents with no selections applied.

*Clicking the **Size** heading and un-checking the selection has the same result.*

17. Close the **Documents** window.

Driving Lesson 31 - Revision

This Driving Lesson covers the features introduced in this section. Try not to refer to the previous Driving Lessons while completing it.

1. Obtain a floppy disk or any other portable storage device.

2. Create a backup copy of the **Reports** folder and all its contents to the floppy disk or another storage device.

3. Create a subfolder within your own named folder (in **My Documents**) and name it **Organisation**.

4. Copy the **Advert** and **CIA Training Ltd - Overview** files from **Reports** into the **Organisation** folder.

5. **Advert** was copied in error. Check that **Advert** is still in the **Reports** folder, then delete it from the **Organisation** folder.

6. Open the **Organisation** folder and rename the **CIA Training Ltd - Overview** as **CIA Background.docx**.

7. Delete your named folder and all of its contents.

8. Delete the **Photograph** file from **2 Managing Files**.

9. **Photograph** has been deleted in error. Restore it from the **Recycle Bin** to its original location.

10. View the **Properties** of **Photograph**. What is shown as the **Modified** date?

11. Find any **Microsoft Word Document** files in the **My Documents** folder that contain the text **sewing machine**. What is the name of the file?

12. Close any open windows.

Answers to this revision exercise can be found at the end of this guide.

If you experienced any difficulty completing this exercise refer back to the Driving Lessons in this section. Then redo the Revision Exercise.

Driving Lesson 32 - Revision

This Driving Lesson covers the features introduced in this section. Try not to refer to the previous Driving Lessons while completing it.

1. Somewhere within the **ECDL** folder are files that have information on advertising. Search the folder for any file containing the text '**advertising**'. One of the files should be from the **Managing Files** folder. What is the name and type of the relevant file?

2. Create a new folder within the supplied **ECDL** folder and call it **Revision**.

3. Search the **2 Managing Files** folder (and its subfolders) for all files that have a **docx** extension.

4. Select all the files from the **Search** dialog box and use any method to copy them all.

5. Select the new **Revision** folder. **Paste** the copied files into this folder.

6. Copy all the files within **Revision** so as to produce duplicates within the same folder. How many files are in the folder?

7. Search for all the files in **2 Managing Files** (and its subfolders) that are between 100KB and 1MB (Medium size), and copy them to the **Revision** folder. How many files are now in the folder?

8. Delete the folder **Revision** including all its contents.

9. Close any open windows.

i *Answers to this revision exercise can be found at the end of this guide.*

If you experienced any difficulty completing this exercise refer back to the Driving Lessons in this section. Then redo the Revision Exercise.

Once you are confident with the features, complete the Record of Achievement Matrix referring to the section at the end of the guide. Only when competent move on to the next Section.

Section 3
Print Management

By the end of this Section you should be able to:

Select a Printer

Set a Default Printer

Add a New Printer

View a Print Job

Control Print Jobs

Understand how to Perform Maintenance

To gain an understanding of the above features, work through the **Driving Lessons** in this **Section**.

For each **Driving Lesson**, read the **Park and Read** instructions, without touching the keyboard, then work through the numbered steps of the **Manoeuvres** on the computer. Complete the **Revision Exercise(s)** at the end of the section to test your knowledge.

Driving Lesson 33 - Printers

▣ Park and Read

The **Printers** window contains icons for each installed printer that is available to the computer, either via a network connection or directly connected. A properties dialog box can be displayed for each printer allowing various settings for the printer to be changed. If more than one printer is available, it is possible to change the default printer.

It is also possible to add a new printer to the selection available. Clicking **Add Printer** starts the **Add Printer Wizard**, which guides the user through the process of setting up a new printer.

Right clicking on a specific printer's icon displays a shortcut menu. Select **See what's printing** to view the **print queue** window for that printer. This window gives information regarding the print jobs that have been sent to that printer and the progress of each job.

⌒ Manoeuvres

1. Click **Start** and select **Control Panel** from the **Start** menu. Select **View Devices and Printers** under **Hardware and Sound**.

Your printer/s will be different to those shown in the diagram

2. This example shows one directly connected printer (**hp deskjet 845c**) and one shared printer connected directly to the network (**HP LaserJet M2727**) available. Notice that the icon for the **hp deskjet** printer includes a default printer symbol, .

continued over

Driving Lesson 33 - Continued

3.   The **HPLaserJet** icon includes a **heads** symbol to indicate that the printer is shared.

HP LaserJet
M2727 MFP
Series PS

4.   To make a different printer the default, right click the required printer and select **Set as default printer** from the shortcut menu.

5.   Right click on a printer icon and select **Printer properties** from the menu.

HP LaserJet M2727 MFP Series PS Properties

Security		Device Settings		About
General	Sharing	Ports	Advanced	Color Management

HP LaserJet M2727 MFP Series PS

Location:

Comment:

Model: HP LaserJet M2727 MFP Series PS

Features
Color: No   Paper available:
Double-sided: Yes   A4
Staple: No
Speed: 27 ppm
Maximum resolution: 1200 dpi

Preferences...   Print Test Page

OK   Cancel   Apply

i *The tabs available in the **Properties** dialog box will depend on the type of printer selected.*

6.   Click each of the tabs at the top of the **Properties** dialog box to see which aspects of the printer operation can be changed. **General** gives general information about the printer. The **Preferences** button on this tab allows features such as paper orientation and size to be controlled. The other tabs control all other aspects associated with the printer, e.g. **Sharing**. Examine the options then close the dialog box.

7.   If possible, ensure that a directly connected printer is defined as the default printer.

8.   Leave the **Devices and Printers** window open for the next Driving Lesson.

Driving Lesson 34 - Add a New Printer

 Park and Read

If a new printer is made available, its details must be added to the computer before it can be used. An **Add Printer** wizard is available to make the task easier. *Windows 7* also has a powerful auto-detect system which will detect and add the details for most printers automatically. *Windows* will automatically add details for a local printer connected using a **USB** port.

Manoeuvres

These actions can be read for information now but should only be followed when a new printer is connected or the icon for an existing printer is lost.

1.   Click the ⬚Add a printer⬚ button on the **Devices and Printers** window toolbar to start the **Add Printer** wizard.

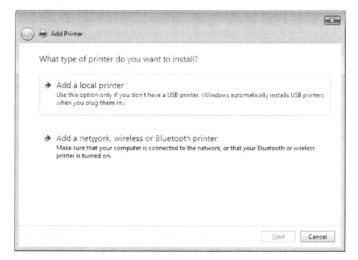

2.   Select which type of printer is being added, either **Local** (directly connected to your computer) or **Networked** (connected to another computer on the network or directly connected to the network).

3.   For a network printer, go to step 7. For a local printer, select the port the printer is connected to, (usually **LPT1**). Click **Next**.

4.   Select the **Manufacturer and model** of your printer. If the **Drivers** for the printer are on a disk, click **Have Disk** and follow the instructions. Click **Next**.

continued over

Driving Lesson 34 - Continued

5.   Enter a name for the printer. This is the name that appears with the printer icon and identifies this printer whenever printer selection is required. There is an option here to set this printer as the default.

6.   Click **Next**. An icon for the new printer icon is added to the **Devices and Printers** window. Request a **test page** print if required and click **Finish**. Go to step **10**.

ℹ️   *Most local printers connected using a **USB** port will be detected automatically, there will be no need to use the **Add printer** wizard.*

ℹ️   *See the **Printer Maintenance** Driving Lesson for more information about installing and updating printer drivers.*

7.   For a **Network** printer, *Windows* will display details of all available printers that it can find.

8.   Either select one of the detected printers or click the **isn't listed** option and find the printer manually, by browsing or entering a known path.

ℹ️   *Password authorisation may be required to access other computers on the network.*

9.   Click **Next**. Enter a name for the printer. Click **Next**. The new printer icon is added. Request a **test page** print if required and click **Finish**.

ℹ️   *To remove a printer icon from the **Printers** window, right click on it and select **Remove Device** from the shortcut menu. There will be a message to confirm the choice.*

10. Leave the **Devices and Printers** window open for the next Driving Lesson.

Driving Lesson 35 - Print Jobs

▐ Park and Read

It is possible to view and control the status of a print job.

⌐ Manoeuvres

1. From the **Devices and Printers** window, double click on the icon of the default printer for your computer. A window is displayed, with the default printer name, listing any documents printing or waiting to be printed on this printer. This is sometimes called the **print queue** window.

Document Name	Status	Owner	Pages	Size	Sul

hp deskjet 845c series
Printer   Document   View

ℹ️ *There will be no documents in the list if there are no current printing jobs or jobs waiting to print.*

ℹ️ *Depending on the system being used you may not be allowed to control the printer at all. This is most likely to happen with a networked printer, or if you do not have administrator status. In this case either switch off the printer to temporarily disable it, or read the rest of this exercise for information only.*

2. To demonstrate controlling print jobs it will be convenient to temporarily pause the printer operation. Select **Printer**, then select **Pause Printing**. The word **Paused** should appear on the **Title Bar**.

hp deskjet 845c series - Paused

3. To quickly create a print job, first display the contents of the **2 Managing Files** folder in the **Documents** window.

4. Right click on **Notepad file** and select **Print** from the shortcut menu. Close the **2 Managing Files** window.

5. Redisplay the **print queue** window and in a few seconds a print job will appear. It will stay there because the printer operation has been paused.

continued over

Driving Lesson 35 - Continued

ℹ️ *If the printer is not paused, the job will print and be removed from the queue almost immediately.*

6.   Note the information about the print job that is displayed.

7.   As well as controlling the printer, individual print jobs can be controlled from this window. Click on the **Notepad file** job to select it, then select **Document** from the **Menu bar**.

8.   Select **Pause** from the menu. The status of the job changes to **Paused**. If the printer was active, printing of this job would stop and the next print job on the queue would be printed.

9.   With the **Notepad file** still highlighted, select **Document** again. Select **Resume** and the job would resume printing from where it paused.

10.   With the **Notepad file** still highlighted, select **Document** then **Restart**. If the printer was active, printing of this job would start again from the beginning.

11.   With the **Notepad file** still highlighted, select **Document** then **Cancel**. Click **Yes** to confirm the action. The print job is permanently removed from the queue. A job can be cancelled if it is waiting in the queue or currently printing. Cancelling a job that is printing will terminate the print and allow any subsequent jobs in the queue to start.

ℹ️ *Some printers have an internal memory which stores currently printing pages, so that sometimes printing can still continue for a time after a job is cancelled.*

12.   To reactivate the printer, select **Printer**, then select **Pause Printing**. The word **Paused** will disappear from the **printers** title bar to confirm that the printer is active again.

ℹ️ *If you have the necessary authority, all jobs can be removed from the print queue by selecting **Printer** then **Cancel All Documents**. This is sometimes known as **purging** print jobs.*

13.   Close the **printer** window but leave the **Devices and Printers** window open.

Driving Lesson 36 - Printer Maintenance

▣ Park and Read

There are various maintenance tasks that will need to be performed from time to time when you use a printer. You will probably need to align ink cartridges after installing or replacing one, but you may also need to do this if printed characters are improperly formed, or are misaligned at the left margin, or when vertical, straight lines look wavy. You may need to print a test page to check if a printer is printing text and graphics correctly. A test page also shows information such as the printer name, model and driver software version, which can help you troubleshoot printer problems. With a new printer, the driver may need installing, or updating in an older printer.

Other tasks that you will probably have to deal with include replacing consumables, such as paper and toner cartridges, and possibly clearing a paper jam. Basic instructions for these tasks are given below - you <u>may</u> need to refer to manufacturer's guidelines.

To print a test page

Click the **Start** button and open the **Control Panel**. Select **View devices and printers** under **Hardware and Sound**. Right click on your printer and select **Printer properties**. On the **General** tab, look toward the bottom of the dialog box, click [Print **T**est Page] and your printer will automatically print it for you.

To replace an ink cartridge

If your printer uses ink cartridges you will be prompted to replace them as and when they run out. Open the printer lid, the cartridges are automatically moved to the centre for easy access. Remove the old ink cartridge. Get the new cartridge out of the box, take off the protective tape. Insert the new cartridge, pushing into place. Close the lid and the cartridges are automatically moved back to the start position.

continued over

Driving Lesson 36 - Continued

To align cartridges

If you have just installed a new ink cartridge, you may be prompted by the printer software to align it. This will involve a number of simple steps such as printing test sheets and selecting options and will vary for different printers. Follow the instructions given until the process is complete. If necessary, the alignment process can be started from *Windows*. Click the **Start** button and open the **Control Panel**. Select **View devices and printers** under **Hardware and Sound**. Right click on your printer and select **Printing preferences**. There will be an option on one of the tabs to **Align Print Cartridge** or **Print Head Alignment**, or something similar. Choose this option and follow the instructions.

To replace a toner cartridge

If you use a laser printer and the quality isn't as good as it used to be, you may need to replace the toner cartridge. Open the printer door and lift up the hand hold, then remove the old toner cartridge. Get the new cartridge out of the box and give it a gentle shake. Take off the protective tape. Insert the new cartridge, pushing down to ensure it's properly in place.

To replace paper

In a laser printer, slide out the paper drawer, insert the new paper (normally under a metal guard and push the drawer back in. Inkjet printers will normally just need paper inserting in the top or the front.

To clear a paper jam

A paper jam is indicated by a flashing warning light on the printer. First, turn the printer off and on again to see if this will clear the jam. If not, turn the printer off. Remove the paper trays and check for damaged paper. Open any doors, i.e. toner/ink and if necessary remove the toner or ink cartridge to check for paper stuck behind them. Remove any jammed paper by pulling firmly but gently, so it doesn't tear. If it does tear, try turning the rollers to free the paper. Replace paper trays and toner or ink cartridges if they've been removed, close any open doors and turn on the printer. If the paper jam light is still flashing, repeat the process.

To install and update printer drivers

A driver is software that allows a computer to control a printer. Some drivers are included in *Windows*, others are installed when you install the printer. Sometimes you'll need to install drivers using the CD that came with the printer. If there is no CD, go to the printer manufacturer's website and download and install the drivers from there.

If new printer drivers come available then they should be automatically updated via *Windows Update*.

Driving Lesson 37 - Revision

This Driving Lesson covers the features introduced in this section. Try not to refer to the previous Driving Lessons while completing it.

1. The **Devices and Printers** window should still be open. If not, open it.

2. View the **Properties** dialog box for the default printer. What paper size is currently selected? Cancel the **Properties** box.

3. How do you change the default printer?

4. Use the **Help** feature to find information about **printers**.

5. Find a topic about **change your default printer**.

6. Use the **Print** button, , in the **Help** window to print a copy of the article.

7. Close **Help**.

8. Display the **printer queue** for each printer in the **Devices and Printers** window in turn. Are there any current jobs?

9. Close any open windows.

10. When might you need to align print cartridges?

Answers to this revision exercise can be found at the end of this guide.

If you experienced any difficulty completing the Revision, refer back to the Driving Lessons in this section. Then redo the Revision.

Once you are confident with the features, complete the Record of Achievement Matrix referring to the section at the end of the guide. Only when competent move on to the next Section.

Section 4
Running Applications

By the end of this Section you should be able to:

Start and Close an Application

Enter Text

Save and Print Information

Capture Screen Images

Install and Remove Applications

Switch Between Applications

Create and Use Desktop Icons

To gain an understanding of the above features, work through the **Driving Lessons** in this **Section**.

For each **Driving Lesson**, read the **Park and Read** instructions, without touching the keyboard, then work through the numbered steps of the **Manoeuvres** on the computer. Complete the **Revision Exercise(s)** at the end of the section to test your knowledge.

Driving Lesson 38 - Run an Application

▣ Park and Read

When a program is installed on the computer, it normally adds itself somewhere into the **Start** button menus. It may add a new item under **Programs**, or join in with another group of files.

⌐ Manoeuvres

1. Select **Start | All Programs | Accessories | WordPad**. This application is a simple word processor. Documents can be opened, edited, formatted, printed, saved and used by other word processors.

Quick Action Toolbar

Ribbon

Title bar

Ruler

Status bar

2. The application opens in a window which can be moved, resized, scrolled, minimized and closed like any other window. The **Title bar** across the top of the window displays the **Quick Action Toolbar**, the application name and the current open file, **Document** by default.

3. *WordPad* has a **Ribbon** across the top of the screen. This includes tabs **Home** and **View**. Each tab consists of groups of buttons to perform tasks.

4. There is a **Ruler** along the top of the document and a **Status bar** along the bottom.

5. If the **Ruler** or **Status bar** is not visible, then click the **View** tab and check the appropriate option.

continued over

Driving Lesson 38 - Continued

6. The **Home** tab is displayed by default. Take note of the available groups, **Clipboard**, **Font**, **Paragraph**, **Insert**, **Editing** and the buttons within them.

*As the mouse pointer is moved over a button in a group, a **ToolTip** appears, describing the action associated with each.*

7. Display the **View** tab. Repeat the process of displaying the **Tooltips** for the buttons contained on the **View** tab.

8. Click the **WordPad Help** button, (found under the **Close** button on the right side top corner of the screen), to open the **Windows Help and Support** window.

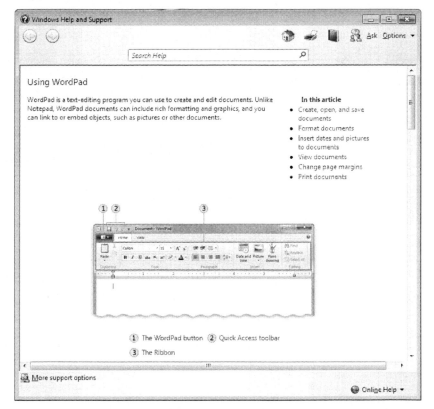

9. Browse through the help system to learn more about the capabilities of *WordPad* by clicking the blue hyperlinked text.

10. Close the **Help** window by clicking the **Close** button, in the window.

11. Leave *WordPad* open for the next Driving Lesson.

Driving Lesson 39 - Entering & Formatting Text

▣ Park and Read

WordPad uses a flashing cursor to show where the text is entered and edited. The cursor can be moved by clicking the mouse pointer or by using the cursor (arrow) keys on the keyboard. Text is entered at the cursor position and has wordwrap, so that when the edge of the paper is reached, the text automatically wraps on to the next line.

The font, font style, size and colour of text can be changed by using the buttons in the **Font** group on the **Home** tab.

⌒ Manoeuvres

1. Enter the following text into *WordPad*, use the <**Enter**> key to start a new paragraph:

    CIA Training Ltd is a specialist publishing company, based in the North East of England. It has been trading for over twenty years and has recently moved to new, larger premises in Sunderland.

    The company is involved in the production of computer training materials. More details are available by telephoning (0191) 549 5002.

2. Select the first sentence, beginning **CIA Training Ltd**, by clicking and dragging the mouse pointer over the text, so that it is highlighted.

3. Press <**Delete**> to remove the text.

4. To cancel the deletion, click the **Undo** button, 🔄, on the **Quick Access Toolbar**, found on the left side of the **Title bar**.

5. Click after **larger premises in Sunderland.** and type in **These premises are located within the Business and Innovation Centre on the north bank of the River Wear.**

6. Select the first sentence again, then on the **Home** tab, locate the **Font** group. Click the arrow at the right of the **Font family** selector to display a list of available fonts. As you move the cursor down the list the text changes to show the effect of the new font. Click to select a different font.

7. In a similar manner, change the font size, font style (bold, italic or underline) and colour of the selected text using the buttons in the **Font** group.

8. Practise formatting text, then leave *WordPad* open for the next Driving Lesson.

Driving Lesson 40 - Saving Text

▣ Park and Read

Documents created in *WordPad* can be saved on to the hard disk or any other storage media to be used again. *WordPad* can only have one document open at a time, so any open document will be closed before another is opened. If the document has not been saved there will be a prompt to save it then.

↱ Manoeuvres

1.   To save the document click the *WordPad* button, ■▼ and select **Save as**. The **Save As** dialog box is shown.

ℹ️ *Alternatively, click the **Save button**, 🖫 on the **Quick Access Toolbar** or the key press <**Ctrl S**> to display the **Save As** dialog box.*

2.   The **Folders** section of the dialog box works in the same way as the **Navigation pane** described in earlier exercises. Navigate through this view to display the contents of the **Reports** folder created earlier. The path is **CIA DATA FILES/ECDL/2 Managing Files/Reports**.

3.   The contents of the **Reports** folder will be shown on the right, and part of the path will be shown in the **Address bar** at the top of the dialog box.

ℹ️ *It is important to realise that the folder is not empty. However, it contains none of the selected file types (.rtf). This is an important distinction.*

continued over

Driving Lesson 40 - Continued

4. From **Save as type** make sure **Rich Text Format (RTF)** is selected and enter the **File name** as **WordPad Document**. Click the **Save** button to save this file to the specified folder.

5. Change the text **CIA** to **ABC**.

6. To open another document click the **WordPad** button then **Open**.

i *Alternatively, press <**Ctrl O**> to display the **Open** dialog box.*

7. Check that the **2 Managing Files** folder is being displayed, and change the file type to **All Documents**. Click on the file **Notepad file**.

File name:	Notepad file.txt	▼	All Documents (*.*)	▼
			Open ▼	Cancel

8. Click on the **Open** button. The document that was open is closed automatically. There will be a prompt to save the changes to the original document.

> **WordPad** ✕
>
> Do you want to save changes to C:\Users\Trainer\Documents\CIA DATA FILES\ECDL\2 Managing Files\Reports\WordPad Document.rtf?
>
> Save   Don't Save   Cancel

9. Select **Don't Save** to ignore the changes.

10. **Notepad file** will now be opened and visible on screen. Use formatting tools to change the appearance of the document.

11. Place a blank floppy disk in the disk drive or attach a removable storage device, click the **WordPad** button then select **Save as**.

12. Change the **File name** to **Cia2**, and the location to the removable storage device.

13. The original file type was **Text Document** but as formatting has been applied, the file must now be saved as a **Rich Text Format** document. Use the drop down list in **Save as type** to select **Rich Text Format (RTF)**. Click Save .

14. Leave the document open for the next Driving Lesson.

Driving Lesson 41 - Print a Document

▣ Park and Read

It is an easy task to print out documents from *WordPad*. The printing margins can be set from the **Page Setup** dialog box. Page layout can be previewed before printing within **Print Preview**. A picture of the printed page will appear, along with the margins that have been set.

☞ Manoeuvres

1. With **Cia2** open, click the **WordPad** button then select **Page Setup**.

2. Change the four values of the margins to **50mm** (delete the existing values and retype as **50**). Click **OK** when finished.

3. Click the **WordPad** button and place the mouse cursor over **Print** (do not click on **Print**) move to the right and click on **Print Preview**.

continued over

Driving Lesson 41 - Continued

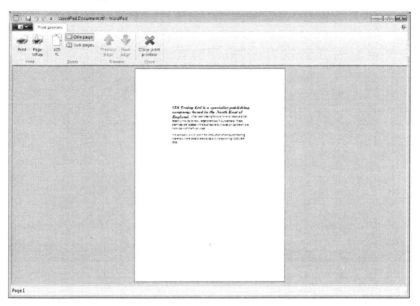

4. Click the magnifier cursor on the document to zoom in to take a closer look.

i *If the document runs to more than one page then **Next page** and **Previous page** buttons can be used. **Two pages** shows two pages of the document at once.*

5. Click the **Print** button, in the **Print Preview** window.

i *Alternatively, from the **Normal** view, click the **WordPad** button then **Print** or the key press <**Ctrl P**>.*

6. Select to print **1** copy of **All** pages. Check that your printer is set up, connected and on-line. Click **Print**.

7. *WordPad* keeps the margins as set (50 from step 2) and keeps the settings, even after *WordPad* is closed. Also, saved documents when opened will have the 50mm margins imposed on them. Display **Page Setup** and use the diagram on the previous page to change the margins back to their default values, i.e. **31.8** top and bottom and **25.4** for left and right.

8. Click the **Save** button, on the **Quick Access Toolbar** to save the document.

9. Leave *WordPad* open for the next exercise.

Driving Lesson 42 - Using Print Screen

▣ Park and Read

An image of any screen display can be captured using the **Print Screen** button then used in another application. For example a screen image (sometimes called a screen shot or screen dump) can be added to a document in a word processing application and then printed out. Moving images on a screen will not be captured.

⌒ Manoeuvres

1.   Minimise the *WordPad* window and display the **Documents** window.

2.   Press **<Print Screen>**, found at the top right of the keyboard. This stores an image of the current screen in an area of the computer known as the **Clipboard**.

> ℹ️ *Capture an image of an active window by holding down <**Alt**> while pressing <**Print Screen**>.*

3.   Close the **Documents** window and click the **WordPad** button, on the **Taskbar** to redisplay the *WordPad* screen containing the document, **Cia2.rtf**.

4.   Click the **WordPad** button then select **New** to start a new document.

5.   The current document is automatically closed. If a **Save changes...** message appears, select **Don't Save**.

6.   At the top of the new document, type the line **This shows the contents of my Documents Library**. Press <Enter> to start a new line.

7.   Click the **Paste** button, Paste. The image is pasted into the document between the margins.

8.   Display **Page Setup** and select **Landscape** (if available) as the **Orientation**. Click **OK**. The page is rotated.

9.   Click on the image, there will be small square "handles" around it.

10.   Click and drag the handle in the bottom right corner diagonally down and right for a few centimetres to increase the size of the image until it fits on a single page.

11.   Check that your printer is set up and connected. Print a single copy of the document.

> ℹ️ *The document with the screen image could be saved now using **Save As**.*

12.   Leave *WordPad* open for the next Driving Lesson.

Driving Lesson 43 - Switch between Applications

Park and Read

More than one application can be open at the same time. The **Taskbar** shows the applications currently running and makes it easy to switch between them.

Manoeuvres

1. If the *WordPad* window is maximised, click the **Restore Down** button, ⟦⟧. The button is replaced by the **Maximize** button, ⟦⟧.

2. The application is now displayed in a smaller window. The sizing and scaling techniques practised earlier apply to all windows. Reduce the size of the window by clicking and dragging the bottom right corner, inwards.

3. Select **Start** button then **All Programs | Accessories | Calculator**. The Calculator accessory opens.

i   *There are four different views of the calculator, **Standard**, **Scientific**, **Programmer** and **Statistics**. Select the required view by clicking **View** on the menu and selecting the appropriate menu choice. The calculator can be operated by clicking on the buttons with the mouse, or by using the keyboard.*

4. Start the **Paint** application from within **Accessories** in the same way.

continued over

Driving Lesson 43 - Continued

5.   All three applications are running. Look at the **Taskbar**. There are buttons for each one.

6.   Click ⬜ for each open window in turn to minimise them.

7.   Look at the **Taskbar**. The **Start** menu button is first, followed by 3 buttons that are applications that have been permanently placed (pinned) there. The last 3 buttons are for each open application. This shows that the new 3 applications are still open in the background.

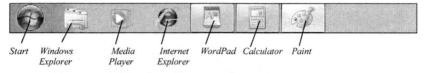

| | *Windows* | | *Media* | *Internet* | | | |
| *Start* | *Explorer* | | *Player* | *Explorer* | *WordPad* | *Calculator* | *Paint* |

8.   Click on the **WordPad** button on the **Taskbar**.

9.   *WordPad* opens and becomes the active window.

10. Now click on **Calculator** on the **Taskbar**. This becomes the active window (the **Title Bar** becomes darker). Try a few calculations. Use both the mouse and the keyboard. Select **View | Scientific** to switch modes.

11. The *WordPad* window can still be seen, even though it's not the active window. Click once on the *WordPad* window to make it active.

12. All currently open windows are shown as icons. Click the **Paint** icon to make that the active window.

13. Leave all the applications open.

Driving Lesson 44 - Closing an Application

▣ Park and Read

Applications shown on the **Taskbar** by a button are still open. To remove an application it must be closed. There are various methods to close down an active application.

Sometimes however an application can become 'stuck' and not respond to any of its buttons or commands. In such an emergency there is a way that *Windows* can close the application down.

☞ Manoeuvres

1.   Make **Calculator** the active window by clicking its button on the **Taskbar**.

2.   Close the **Calculator** by clicking the **Close** button (top right).

| Calculator | | □ | ▭ | ✕ | *Close button* |

View   Edit   Help

$$0$$

⦿ Degrees	◯ Radians		◯ Grads		MC	MR	MS	M+	M-
	Inv	ln	(	)	←	CE	C	±	√
Int	sinh	sin	x^2	n!	7	8	9	/	%
dms	cosh	cos	x^y	$\sqrt[y]{x}$	4	5	6	*	1/x
π	tanh	tan	x^3	$\sqrt[y]{x}$	1	2	3	-	=
F-E	Exp	Mod	log	10^x	0	.	+		

3.   The next window is brought to the front and displayed.

4.   Make *WordPad* active, then click the **WordPad** button and select **Exit**. Do not save the document if prompted. The application will close.

5.   Assuming that **Paint** needs to be shut down but is not responding to the **Close** button or the **Exit** command, right click on a blank area of the **Taskbar** and select **Start Task Manager** from the shortcut menu. Alternatively, press and hold down <**Ctrl Alt**>, press <**Delete**>, then select **Start Task Manager**.

continued over

Driving Lesson 44 - Continued

6. The **Windows Task Manager** window is displayed. Make sure the **Applications** tab is selected. All current applications are listed. The **Status** column indicates if the application is **Running** or **Not responding**.

7. Select the **Paint** task and click **End Task**. The application will be shut down. If the application is waiting for a response there will be a confirmation message and you will need to click **End Task**.

ℹ️ *If there is unsaved data in the application you may be given the option to save the data before proceeding.*

ℹ️ *This method must NOT be used as a normal close down method. Data in use may be corrupted or lost.*

8. Close the **Windows Task Manager** window.

Driving Lesson 45 - Install/Uninstall an Application

▣ Park and Read

Most *Windows* applications include programs that will control their installation process automatically. The user may then have to select from menu options and will usually have to make choices from a series of Wizard screens. These will typically ask where the application is to be installed and maybe what optional features are required. When the screens are completed, the application will be installed. *Windows 7* can also handle manual program installation and removal by using **Programs** in the **Control Panel**.

⌒ Manoeuvres

1. Place the required application CD/DVD or floppy in the appropriate drive. Depending on the **AutoPlay** settings in *Windows 7* you may be asked if you want to run the installation program, for example:

or

ℹ️ *In order to see the **AutoPlay** settings, open the **Control Panel** window from the **Start** menu, click **Hardware and Sound** then click **AutoPlay**.*

2. If you are sure you want to install the program, click the **run** option and follow the on screen instructions.

3. If *Windows* cannot find the installation program, use the **Open folder** option to search for it manually. The name of the program, e.g. **setup.exe**, will usually be given with the installation instructions.

    General options
    Open folder to view files
    using Windows Explorer

4. To remove an application, open the **Control Panel** window from the **Start** menu and click **Uninstall a program** under **Programs**.

5. Click on the required application to select it then click the **Uninstall/Change** button.

6. Depending on the application, it may be removed immediately (after a confirmation prompt), or there may be more choices to select. Answer any queries and follow the instructions until the application is removed.

ℹ️ *Deleting the relevant files and folders will not remove an application correctly.*

7. Close any open dialog boxes and windows.

Driving Lesson 46 - Create Desktop Icons

▣ Park and Read

Icons called **Shortcuts** can be easily created on the **Desktop**. A **Shortcut** is rather like a "sign post" which points to an object which is in a different place. A commonly used file may be hidden in a folder many layers down on the hard disk, requiring many mouse clicks to get to it. A shortcut to this file may be created and placed in a convenient place, such as on the **Desktop** itself. When the shortcut icon is double clicked, the file is opened immediately. Shortcuts may point to files, folders or programs.

⌐ Manoeuvres

1. To create a shortcut for the **Calculator**, select **Start | All Programs | Accessories**.

2. Move the mouse over **Calculator** and right click. From the shortcut menu, select **Send To**.

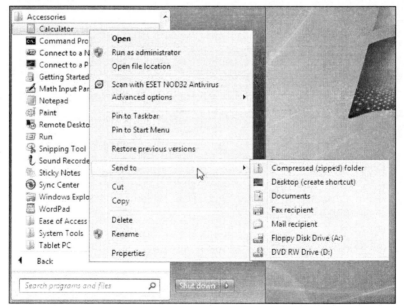

3. Select **Desktop (create shortcut)**.

4. Click anywhere on a clear part of the **Desktop** to remove the menus.

continued over

Driving Lesson 46 - Continued

5. A new icon appears on the **Desktop**. Double click on it to start the **Calculator** application.

6. Close the **Calculator** window.

7. To delete the shortcut, right click on the **Calculator** icon on the **Desktop** and select **Delete**, then **Yes** to confirm.

8. Shortcuts can be created to any folder or file. Open the **Documents** window, and expand **Documents** in the **Navigation pane** to show the contents of the **ECDL** folder.

9. Right click **2 Managing Files**. From the shortcut menu, select **Send To**, then **Desktop (create shortcut)**.

10. Close the **Documents** window to see the **Desktop**. A new folder icon has appeared on the **Desktop**. Right click the icon and select **Rename** from the menu.

11. Type **Course Data** and press <**Enter**> to replace the highlighted name.

12. Double click the **Course Data** icon to open the folder and display the contents of the **2 Managing Files** folder.

13. Right click **Notepad file** and from the shortcut menu, select **Send To**, then **Desktop (create shortcut)**.

14. Close the folder display. A new file icon appears on the **Desktop**. Notice that the appearance of an icon depends on what type of object it is.

15. Using icons as shortcuts to files is covered in the next Driving Lesson.

Driving Lesson 47 - Use Desktop Icons

▣ Park and Read

Double clicking on an icon for a program will start that program.

Double clicking on an icon for a folder will open that folder.

Double clicking on an icon for a file will start an application that will open the file. The application used depends on the type of file, which is defined by the file extension. So for example, double clicking an icon for a **.docx** file will start *Word*, double clicking an **.xlsx** file will start *Excel*. This is why it is important to maintain the correct file extensions when copying or renaming files.

If *Windows* does not know which application to use to open a file, it will offer to look it up on the Web or prompt the user to select one from a list such as this:

⌒ Manoeuvres

1. Double click on the **Notepad file** shortcut icon created in the last Driving Lesson. The **Notepad** application will start and **Notepad file** will be opened ready for editing or other processes.

2. Close the **Notepad** application.

3. Create shortcut icons for other files in the **2 Managing Files** folder and double click them to see which applications start.

4. Use right click and **Delete** to remove all the shortcut icons created in both this Driving Lesson and the last one.

Driving Lesson 48 - Revision

This Driving Lesson covers the features introduced in this section. Try not to refer to the previous Driving Lessons while completing it.

1.   Create a **Desktop** shortcut to the **Paint** accessory.

2.   Create a **Desktop** shortcut to the *Windows Media Player*.

3.   Rename the shortcut **Media Player**.

4.   Use the shortcuts to open both applications.

5.   Practise switching between them using the **Taskbar**.

6.   Start *WordPad* and create a small letter inviting a friend to a party.

7.   Print the letter.

8.   Save the letter in **2 Managing Files** folder as **Party**.

9.   Close *WordPad*.

10.   Close the other two open applications.

11.   Delete both the **Desktop** shortcuts.

If you experienced any difficulty completing this exercise, refer back to the Driving Lessons in this section. Then redo the Revision Exercise.

Once you are confident with the features, complete the Record of Achievement Matrix referring to the section at the end of the guide. Only when competent move on to the next Section.

Section 5
Using Compress

By the end of this Section you should be able to:

Understand File Compression

Compress Files

Extract Compressed Files

To gain an understanding of the above features, work through the **Driving Lessons** in this **Section**.

For each **Driving Lesson**, read the **Park and Read** instructions, without touching the keyboard, then work through the numbered steps of the **Manoeuvres** on the computer. Complete the **Revision Exercise(s)** at the end of the section to test your knowledge.

Driving Lesson 49 - File Compression

▣ Park and Read

Modern computer applications often involve very large files. Multimedia files in particular, e.g. images, videos and sound, can occupy megabytes of space. This can create problems of storage and more importantly, of transferring such large files. Sending megabytes of data as an e-mail attachment or downloading enormous files from the Internet can be tedious or impractical.

Fortunately programs exist which are able to compress files down to a fraction of their original size so that they can be stored or transmitted much more easily. The files cannot be used in their compressed state, but must be uncompressed (using the same program) before use.

Another feature of compression software is that it can compress several files into a single folder, which makes handling the compressed files even easier.

For example, the **ECDL** folder should now have properties similar to this:

	ECDL
Type:	File folder
Location:	C:\Users\Ian Chapman\Documents\CIA DATA FILE
Size:	7.37 MB (7,733,222 bytes)
Size on disk:	7.57 MB (7,942,144 bytes)
Contains:	123 Files, 7 Folders

Over a hundred files in several folders occupying over **7 MB**.

By using compression, all these files can be compressed (zipped) to a single archive folder of about **4 MB**.

Name	Date	Type	Size
ECDL.zip	13/11/2009 14:38	Compressed (zipped) Folder	4,159 KB

This file can be easily transmitted to another user who can then uncompress (unzip) it and so recreate the original files on their computer.

Windows 7 has the compressing/uncompressing feature built in. Earlier versions of *Windows* may require the installation of a separate program such as **WinZip**.

Driving Lesson 50 - Compress Files

▣ Park and Read

Windows 7 contains a basic file compression feature so there is no need to install any additional programs. There are, however, other stand-alone file compression programs which could be used.

Windows creates compressed files in folders with **.zip** extensions. Further files can be added to the **.zip** folder and they will automatically be compressed. The process of compressing files this way is sometimes called **zipping** because of the file extension of the final folder. The compressed files are often called **zipped** files.

If folders are zipped, all content including subfolders will be compressed into the **.zip** folder.

⌒ Manoeuvres

1.   Open the **Documents** window from the **Start Menu**.

2.   Open **CIA DATA FILES**, then **ECDL**, and finally display the contents of the **2 Managing Files** folder.

3.   Click on the **Clothing** file to select it, hold down the <**Ctrl**> key and click on the **Contents** file.

4.   With both files selected, right click on either of them and select **Send To**.

5.   Select the **Compressed (zipped) folder** option.

Send to	▶	Compressed (zipped) folder
Cut		Desktop (create shortcut)
Copy		Documents
		Fax recipient
Create shortcut		Mail recipient
Delete		Floppy Disk Drive (A:)
Rename		DVD RW Drive (D:)
Properties		

6.   A new folder is created with a **.zip** extension. Rename the folder as **Pack**.

7.   Double click on the **Pack.zip** folder to display its contents. It contains compressed copies of the two files.

continued over

Driving Lesson 50 - Continued

Name	Type	Compressed size	Password ...	Ratio	Size
Clothing.docx	Microsoft Office Word Doc...	9 KB	No	25%	11 KB
Contents.docx	Microsoft Office Word Doc...	8 KB	No	25%	11 KB

i *The file display above may look different as it can be customised. Click and drag column borders to resize them. Click and drag column headers to change the order. Right click a column header to change which columns are displayed or hidden.*

8.   More files can be added to the **zipped** folder at any time. Display the contents of the **2 Managing Files** folder.

9.   Use click and drag (or any other method) to copy the **Mailing** file into the **Pack.zip** folder.

10.   Display the contents of the **Pack.zip** folder again.

Name	Type	Compressed size	Password ...	Size	Ratio
Clothing.docx	Microsoft Office Word Do...	9 KB	No	11 KB	25%
Contents.docx	Microsoft Office Word Do...	8 KB	No	11 KB	25%
Mailing.accdb	Microsoft Office Access 2...	13 KB	No	288 KB	96%

11.   Notice that because the **Mailing** file has been added to a **zipped** folder, it has been automatically compressed.

12.   This **zipped** folder can be processed like any other, i.e. moved, copied, renamed, deleted. For example it could be sent as an e-mail attachment (size about 30KB) and unzipped by the recipient to obtain the original content (size about 300KB).

13.   Close the **Pack.zip** window.

14.   Stand-alone compression programs are also available. Starting such a program will display a window like this one for **WinRAR**.

15.   Navigate to the appropriate location, select the required folders/files and click **Add** to create a compressed file.

Driving Lesson 51 - Uncompress Files

▣ Park and Read

Before a compressed file can be used, it is advisable to uncompress it. For files and folders compressed by *Windows 7* this is a very easy process.

ⓘ *It is possible to open some zipped files directly, for example a zipped word document can be opened directly in Word 2007 but this is not recommended as saving it again may not be straightforward.*

☞ Manoeuvres

1. Display the contents of the **Pack.zip** folder and click Extract all files .

ⓘ *This dialog box can also be displayed by right clicking on **Pack.zip** and selecting **Extract All** from the shortcut menu. By default the files will be unpacked into a new folder with the same name as the zipped folder (without the .zip extension) and in the same location. The destination folder can be changed either by overtyping the path shown or using the **Browse** button.*

2. Click the **Extract** button. A new **Pack** folder appears in the **2 Managing Files** folder. It contains uncompressed copies of the three files that were compressed originally.

ⓘ *To uncompress a file compressed by standalone programs, double click on the compressed file to start the relevant application, then use the **Extract** button.*

3. Close any open windows.

Driving Lesson 52 - Revision

This Driving Lesson covers the features introduced in this section. Try not to refer to the previous Driving Lessons while completing it.

ℹ️ *This exercise requires the use of a File Compression application. If there is not one installed on the computer, the exercise cannot be completed.*

1. Create a new folder in the **My Documents** folder and name it **Compress**.

2. Move the **Banking** document from the **2 Managing Files** folder to the **ECDL** folder.

3. Select all the content of the **2 Managing Files** folder and compress it.

4. Rename the new zipped folder **Revision.zip** and move it to the **Compress** folder.

5. What is the size of **Revision.zip** and of the original **2 Managing Files** folder?

6. Copy the **Banking** document from the **ECDL** folder into the **Revision.zip** folder.

7. Extract all the files in **Revision.zip** directly into the **Compress** folder. **Hint:-** Delete the **\Revision** part of the path in the **Extract** dialog box.

8. The **Compress** folder should now contain all the files from **2 Managing Files** folder (including the **Banking** document), together with the zipped folder **Revision.zip**.

9. Delete the **Compress** folder and all its contents.

10. Move the **Banking** document file back to the **2 Managing Files** folder from the **ECDL** folder.

11. Close any open windows.

ℹ️ *Answers to this revision exercise can be found at the end of this guide.*

If you experienced any difficulty completing this exercise, refer back to the Driving Lessons in this section. Then redo the Revision Exercise.

Once you are confident with the features, complete the Record of Achievement Matrix referring to the section at the end of the guide. Only when competent move on to the next Section.

Section 6
Virus Control

By the end of this Section you should be able to:

Understand Viruses

Understand Virus Transmission

Understand Anti-Virus Protection

Use Anti-Virus Protection Applications

To gain an understanding of the above features, work through the **Driving Lessons** in this **Section**.

For each **Driving Lesson**, read the **Park and Read** instructions, without touching the keyboard, then work through the numbered steps of the **Manoeuvres** on the computer. Complete the **Revision Exercise(s)** at the end of the section to test your knowledge.

Driving Lesson 53 - Computer Viruses

▣ Park and Read

A computer **virus** is a piece of malicious software code introduced to a computer system, with the ability to spread itself to other computers. This should not be confused with the term **bug**, which describes an error or fault in a piece of software code. The extent of the harm caused by viruses varies enormously.

In many cases the contamination remains unnoticed in its host file until a specific event triggers off its action. Viruses can cause many levels of harm to a computer system. The least harmful might cause slightly odd things to happen to a file, for example if a user typed text into a word processed document on an infected computer, certain letters or words might appear on screen in an unexpected text format. Another manifestation of a relatively harmless virus could be the refusal of an application's software to save files to any area other than a specific folder on the HDD, rather than the desired folder on a disk in the floppy drive. The action that a virus carries out when activated is known as the **payload**.

At the other end of the scale, a virus might lie dormant until the built in clock within a PC reaches a certain time on a certain date, or possibly until the computer has been restarted a certain number of times, and then become active. This type of virus is variously known as a **time bomb** or **logic bomb**. It could then destroy the entire file structure as laid down on the HDD and render the HDD completely useless. If this type of virus infected a network, the effect could be catastrophic.

Macro viruses are those that are added to executable files within an application. The most common of these can occur within the **template** files in Microsoft Word and Excel. This is why a user is sometimes given the option of opening such a file with **macros disabled**. If the macro facility can't run, neither can any virus that might be within it!

continued over

Driving Lesson 53 - Continued

A **worm** is a self replicating computer program, which uses a computer network to send copies of itself within a system to other computers on the network. It's not a virus, but can open a door for a virus to enter. At best, it simply clogs up the system resources.

A **Trojan** is **malware** and its name comes from the story of the Trojan horse, because it is disguised as a link to a file that a user would be particularly tempted to open, e.g. a game or a graphics file. Once the link is opened, the Trojan gains access to the system.

A common type of virus is one that arrives in an **e-mail attachment**, installs itself within the recipient's *Outlook* or **Contacts** address book and automatically e-mails itself to some or all of the e-mail addresses it finds there. These viruses are particularly effective since the recipient may not realise that the virus has arrived or they have spread the infection onwards. The new victims are less likely to be suspicious of attachments e-mailed to them by a known contact.

Viruses can only become active within a system if they are introduced to the system from outside and then subsequently activated.

It therefore follows that the only pathways available to viruses are via **input devices** such as **floppy disks**, **memory sticks**, **CDs** or **DVDs** or the **Internet**. If genuine application software from reputable sources only is installed on a PC, in theory there should be no danger. If, however, disks containing applications or files are borrowed/acquired from dubious or unknown sources, the chance of them containing viruses is much greater. As indicated above, e-mails received with file attachments are now a prime source of viruses and should be treated with particular caution, as should any files downloaded from the **World Wide Web** that have a **.exe** extension. This extension identifies **executable** files, i.e. files that are actual programs that will open up and run. If the file contains a virus, the virus will run with the program!

Driving Lesson 54 - Anti-Virus Protection

⊡ Park and Read

There are two approaches to combat the increasing threat of computer viruses. Firstly, modern operating systems such as *Windows 7* are designed to include as many security features as possible, from built in firewall features to user access settings which always prompt for confirmation before executing any functions which could be even potentially hazardous.

In addition to sophisticated operating systems, it is highly recommended to employ a reliable virus protection application. There are many versions of virus protection software available. Basically these operate in two modes.

Firstly, they can **scan** a computer system for existing viruses. These scans can be started manually or can be put on a schedule so that they run at certain times. All or part of the system can be scanned. Most protection applications also offer the option of removing viruses that are found and reversing their effects where possible. This process is known as **disinfecting**.

Secondly, they can run continuously to **shield** a system from any incoming viruses. Possible sources of viruses such as floppy disks and network connections are automatically checked and reported on if necessary. Some applications extend this cover in certain circumstances by checking e-mail even before it has been processed by the computer.

Unfortunately all virus protection programs currently have an inherent problem. They work by scanning the code in a system and comparing it to a list of all known viruses. If a match is found, a virus has been detected. It follows then that the only viruses a protection system can detect are ones it already knows about. When a new virus first appears, the protection software company must identify it and add it to their list of known viruses. The user must then obtain a copy of this new list to update their system before they are protected against the new virus. So it is not enough to install and run virus protection software, it must be continuously updated.

Most protection applications can be updated by downloading the current virus list (or the new additions to it) via the Internet on a regular basis. Some systems can even transmit new additions to virus lists automatically as they become available. It is worth remembering however that at present, no protection system will detect viruses that have appeared since the virus list was last updated.

continued over

Driving Lesson 54 - Continued

Anti-virus measures

Taking certain basic safety precautions will reduce the chances of infection:

- ◆ Install reliable **anti-virus software** and **update** it regularly.
- ◆ Use the software to carry out **regular scans** of the **entire system**.
- ◆ Use the software to scan **any removable disk** that is placed in a drive on the system **before installing or opening any files** from it.
- ◆ Be conscious about the **source** of any software you use!
- ◆ **Save any files downloaded from the Internet**, either to a floppy disk or to the HDD and **scan them with anti-virus software before opening** them.
- ◆ Be particularly suspicious of **any e-mail messages containing attachments** from an unknown source.
- ◆ Even be suspicious of **any e-mail messages** from an unknown source.
- ◆ **Do not open anything suspicious, virus-scan everything!**

Anti-spam Software

Spam mails are a used by many companies as a way of advertising, as it is relatively easy to do. We all get e-mails about medicines, car insurance, etc. However, apart from being annoying, spam mails can be a way of introducing viruses to your computer. Anti-spam software is an effective way of filtering these unwanted messages and is often included with your anti-virus software.

Firewall

Every computer should have an operational **firewall**. A firewall is effectively a filter that determines what type of traffic is allowed to pass out of the system to the Internet, and into the system from the Internet.

Driving Lesson 55 - Anti-Virus Protection Applications

P **Park and Read**

There are many versions of Virus Protection software available from a range of suppliers. As an example this Driving Lesson will look at one, **NOD32** currently available from **Eset**. This has a Control Centre to control all aspects of the application, or it can be started as an on-demand scan.

You may need assistance with this exercise, as your particular application may vary considerably from this example.

Manoeuvres

1.   Locate and run the Virus Protection Control application on the computer.

     NOD32 Control Center will have been installed as a button, 🔘 on the **Taskbar**, , but could be found as a **Desktop** icon or in the **Start** menu (by clicking **All Programs | Eset | EST NOD32 Antivirus | NOD32 Control Center** for example).

2.   The panel contains all the elements mentioned in the previous lesson.

3.   Click [🔘 Update] in the panel on the left. The options for running the virus signature updates are displayed. It is strongly recommended to have these updated automatically, i.e. whenever updates are available.

                                                                    continued over

Driving Lesson 55 - Continued

4.   If the **Update virus signature database** is not current then click it to update it.

5.   When the **Update virus signature database** is current then click **Computer scan**.

6.   Click **Smart scan**.

7.   When the scan is finished, deal with any problems that the scanner finds, if any and then click **OK**.

8.   Close the window. In this example this only closes the Antivirus window, the virus checker is still running in the background.

9.   Most applications allow individual files to be scanned directly. Display the **Documents** window, display the contents of one of the supplied data folders. Right click on any file. There will be an antivirus option in the shortcut menu, in this example **Scan with ESET NOD32 Antivirus**. Select this option. The **NOD32** scanner window will open and the file is scanned. Click **OK**.

10.   Close any open windows.

Driving Lesson 56 - Revision

This Driving Lesson covers the features introduced in this section. Try not to refer to the previous Driving Lessons while completing it.

Indicate whether each of the statements 1 to 10 is **True** or **False**?

1. Viruses do not cause any real damage.

2. Viruses only affect business computers.

3. A virus can be transmitted via a document on a floppy disk.

4. A virus can be transmitted between computers on a network.

5. A virus can be transmitted via an e-mail.

6. If your computer is working OK then you do not have a virus.

7. The only way to remove a virus is to reformat the entire hard disk.

8. Virus protection software can scan a removable storage device such as a floppy disk or memory stick.

9. Once you install and run virus protection software you will never get another virus.

10. Virus protection can be set to automatically check incoming data.

11. Bill Sticker, the Office Manager at CIA World has said that he will not be installing any Virus Protection software on the Company's computers because '**it will cost too much money**'. From what you know about viruses, write a short report listing some of the possible costs that might be incurred if a virus establishes itself on the computer system in a busy office.

Answers to this revision exercise can be found at the end of this guide.

If you experienced any difficulty completing the Revision, refer back to the Driving Lessons in this section. Then redo the Revision.

Once you are confident with the features, complete the Record of Achievement Matrix referring to the section at the end of the guide. Only when competent move on to the next Section.

Section 7
Control Panel

By the end of this Section you should be able to:

Change Date and Time

Control the Background

Choose a Screen Saver

Select Settings

Control Sound and Multimedia

To gain an understanding of the above features, work through the **Driving Lessons** in this **Section**.

For each **Driving Lesson**, read the **Park and Read** instructions, without touching the keyboard, then work through the numbered steps of the **Manoeuvres** on the computer. Complete the **Revision Exercise(s)** at the end of the section to test your knowledge.

Driving Lesson 57 - Control Panel

▣ Park and Read

The **Control Panel** contains tools that control how the *Windows* environment looks and performs. Any changes made are permanent until changed again. The changes will still be in effect after closing down and restarting *Windows*.

The **Control Panel** shows similar functions grouped together under **Category** headings.

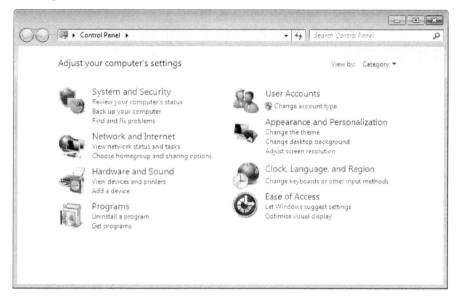

☞ Manoeuvres

1. Click the **Start** button on the **Taskbar**.

2. Select **Control Panel**. The **Control Panel** window appears.

3. Click on the first category heading, **System and Security**.

4. Each of the categories is listed on the left, with **System and Security** selected.

5. There is an option to return to **Control Panel Home**. Click each category in turn and examine the options that are available.

continued over

Driving Lesson 57 - Continued

6.   Select the **Clock, Language and Region** category heading, then select the **Region and Language** from on the right to display the dialog box.

7.   Make sure the **Formats** tab is displayed. Look at the settings here, which control properties such as date, number and currency format. These are controlled by the **Current format** setting which in the UK should be set to **English (United Kingdom)**.

8.   Click the drop down arrow on the **Format** box to see the options but do not change the existing setting.

9.   Select the **Keyboards and Languages** tab and click the **Change keyboards** button. Look at the settings here, which control the **Input Language** and **Keyboard** settings for the system.

10.   The default setting for the UK is **English (United Kingdom) - United Kingdom** for both language and keyboard. Alternative keyboard layouts can be selected by clicking the **Add** button and expanding the **English (United Kingdom)** option. You may need to select **Show More** to see all possible options. It is not recommended to change any settings here, as the keyboard may no longer respond as expected.

11.   Close the current dialog box. Close **Test Services and Input Languages** then close the **Region and Language** dialog box.

12.   Leave the **Control Panel** window open.

Driving Lesson 58 - Date and Time

▣ Park and Read

The computer has a built in clock and calendar. On occasion, the time or date may need to be changed. Modern computers can be set to adjust automatically for the clocks going forward or back. Take care if planning to alter the date or time on a networked computer as the system may need to have all components synchronised.

↱ Manoeuvres

1. If the **Clock, Language and Region** window is not already open, select it from the **Control Panel**, then select **Date and Time**.

2. Click `Change date and time...` to make any changes to the settings. You might be prompted for permission to continue.

3. Use the calendar and digital time displays to change date and time if necessary, then click **OK**. Check before doing this on a network.

ℹ️ *Date and time can also be changed by clicking the **Time** display in the right corner of the **Taskbar**.*

4. Click `Change time zone...` to see if the correct time zone is in use, if not click the drop down arrow and select the correct one.

ℹ️ *The option to **Automatically adjust clock for Daylight Saving Time** is here.*

5. Click **OK** to accept any changes, then close the **Date and Time** dialog box.

Driving Lesson 59 - Display Options

⊞ Park and Read

The *Windows* display can be personalised to suit the user. All the colours, patterns, fonts, etc., used on screen can be changed in a number of ways.

🖑 Manoeuvres

1. In the **Control Panel**, select the **Appearance and Personalization** category.

2. Click **Personalization** to display a list of options.

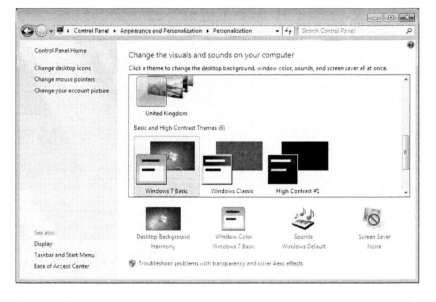

ℹ️ *This **Personalisation** window can also be displayed by right clicking on the **Desktop** and selecting **Personalize** from the shortcut menu.*

3. **Themes**, **Desktop Background**, **Sounds** and **Screen Saver** can all be defined from here. Other settings are available by clicking items in the left pane.

4. Leave the window on screen for the next Driving Lesson.

Driving Lesson 60 - Screen Saver

⊟ Park and Read

A **screen saver** is a moving pattern or message that appears on the screen when the computer hasn't been used for a set period of time. Originally this was to save the screen from having the same picture burned into it. A **log on** can also be set when the screen saver ends to prevent unauthorised use.

↱ Manoeuvres

1. Select the **Screen Saver** icon from the **Personalization** window. A **Screen Saver Settings** dialog box is displayed.

2. Click on the drop down **Screen saver** list and select each available screen saver in turn, noticing the effect in the sample screen. Select **Settings** where relevant to see the options that can be varied.

3. Select **Preview** for a few, to see the effect on the screen (as soon as the mouse is moved the **Preview** will end).

4. Select a **Wait** time. This is the amount of time the computer has to be idle before it activates the screen saver. There is an option to force users to logon again when resuming after the screen saver has been activated.

5. Click **OK** to apply the current settings, or **Cancel** to leave them unchanged.

6. Leave the **Personalization** window open for the next Driving Lesson.

Driving Lesson 61 - Background and Resolution

⊞ Park and Read

Any image can be used as the background to the **Desktop** display.

The resolution of the display screen can be altered to suit the user.

↱ Manoeuvres

1. Select the **Desktop Background** icon in the **Personalization** window.

2. Drop down the list of **Picture location** folders and click some of them to see the images available. If required, select one. You may have to minimize the window to see the effect.

3. Click **Save changes** to select your selection or **Cancel** to leave the settings unchanged to return to the **Personalization** window.

4. Select **Display** from the left, then **Adjust resolution**.

ℹ️ *This window can also be displayed by right clicking on a blank area of the* *Desktop and selecting* *Screen resolution* *from the shortcut menu.*

5. From here it is possible to change the **Resolution**, which defines the pixel resolution of the display. Most of our guides are based on 1024 by 768 pixels but the setting depends on the size of the monitor, the installed video card and the user's preference. Click the **Resolution** drop down to see the available options. Do <u>not</u> change anything.

6. Leave the **Screen Resolution** dialog box open.

Driving Lesson 62 - Colour

▣ Park and Read

The **Window Color** option gives the opportunity to change the look of the *Windows* screens and dialog boxes by altering the colours and fonts associated with individual components. These effects will only be seen when there is no other theme applied. The colour quality settings used by your display can also be accessed, although it is recommended to leave the default settings unchanged.

⌒ Manoeuvres

1. Click **Advanced** settings in the **Screen Resolution** dialog box.

2. Click **List All Modes**. Valid combinations of resolution and colour depth for your monitor can be selected here. Click **Cancel** to retain the current selection, then **Cancel** again to return to **Screen Resolution**.

3. Use the **Back** button twice to return to the **Personalization** window.

4. Select **Window Color** from the **Personalization** window.

5. Click the drop down arrow in the **Item** field and select **Active Title Bar**.

ℹ️ *Alternatively, click the title bar of the **Active Window** in the sample area.*

6. Change the **Color 1**, **Color 2** and the **Font** settings to see the effect.

7. Click **Cancel** to close the **Window Color and Appearance** dialog box without applying any of the changes.

8. Leave the **Personalization** window open for the next exercise.

Driving Lesson 63 - Sound

▣ Park and Read

Sounds can be assigned to various **events** in *Windows* by using the **Sound** dialog box. A list of events is shown, those with sounds attached are indicated by a speaker icon.

ⓘ *Before starting this lesson, the speakers need to be attached, switched on and the volume controls set.*

↱ Manoeuvres

1.　Click the **Sounds** icon in the lower part of the **Personalization** window.

2.　The sound dialog box is displayed. Make sure that the **Sounds** tab is selected. This shows a list of **Program Events**. An icon, 🔊, indicates which events have sounds attached.

3.　Click on the **Critical Stop** event. The **Sounds** box shows that the sound file **Windows Critical Stop.wav** will play when this program event runs.

4.　Click the **Test** button, ▶ **Test**, to hear the sound.

continued over

Driving Lesson 63 - Continued

*By using the drop down list in the **Sounds** box, or by using the **Browse** button, alternative sounds could be attached to this event.*

5.   Click the **Playback** tab to see which audio output devices are available.

6.   Click the **Recording** tab to see which audio input devices (if any) are available.

7.   Click the **Communications** tab to see available options for sound if you are using your PC to make telephone calls.

8.   Close the **Sound** dialog box and the **Control Panel** window.

9.   A simple way to control sound volume is to use the **Volume** control, at the right end of the taskbar. If this icon is not present, right click on a blank area of the **Taskbar** and select **Properties**. Click the **Customize** button under **Notification Area**.

10.   Make sure the **Volume** option is selected under **Icons** as **Show icon and notifications**. Click **OK**, then **OK** again.

11.   Click the **Volume** control on the **Taskbar**. A volume slider control will appear.

12.   Click and drag the slider to vary the sound level.

13.   Click the **Mute Speakers** button, ◀◈, to switch off the sound.

14.   Click on the slider again to cancel the **Mute**.

15.   Click on a blank area of **Desktop** to remove the slider control.

16.   Most applications that play sounds will also have their own built in volume controls. For example, start **Windows Media Player** from the **Start** menu or the **Taskbar**, if it is installed.

Volume slider

17.   The control panel at the bottom of the window includes a volume slider. Move this from side to side when any item is playing to control the sound volume.

Usually the sound output device (speakers or headphones) will have a separate control for volume.

18.   Close the **Windows Media Player**.

Driving Lesson 64 - Revision

This Driving Lesson covers the features introduced in this section. Try not to refer to the previous Driving Lessons while completing it.

1. Check what day your birthday will fall on next year using the **Date and Time** icon on the **Taskbar**.

2. From the **Control Panel**, open the **Desktop Background** window and note the current image.

3. Select a new background image from the samples displayed and minimize the **Desktop Background** window to see the effect.

4. Restore the **Desktop Background** window and click **Cancel**. What happens to the background image?

5. Change the **Screen Saver** to **Mystify**, to come on after **2 minutes**. What button can you press to see the effect immediately?

6. Return to the original **Screen Saver** settings.

7. Make sure you have a speaker icon on the **Taskbar**.

8. Display the **Display** dialog box and note the current **Resolution** setting. Increase the **Resolution**, if possible, otherwise reduce it. Click **OK**. What happens to the size of the **Desktop** icons?

9. Restore the **Resolution** to its original value.

10. If you are listening to music using *Windows Media Player* on your computer, name three possible different ways to control the volume.

11. Close the **Control Panel** window.

| i |

Answers to this revision exercise can be found at the end of this guide.

If you experienced any difficulty completing this exercise, refer back to the Driving Lessons in this section. Then redo the Revision Exercise.

Once you are confident with the features, complete the Record of Achievement Matrix referring to the section at the end of the guide.

Section 8
Systems Maintenance

By the end of this Section you should be able to:

Understand the importance of systems maintenance

Carry out routine maintenance

Know when specialists should carry out maintenance

Identify IT problems and know how to resolve them

To gain an understanding of the above features, work through the **Driving Lessons** in this **Section**.

For each **Driving Lesson**, read the **Park and Read** instructions, without touching the keyboard, then work through the numbered steps of the **Manoeuvres** on the computer. Complete the **Revision Exercise(s)** at the end of the section to test your knowledge.

Driving Lesson 65 - Maintaining Systems

▣ Park and Read

Routine maintenance keeps your computer healthy. *Windows* has various tools that help to keep your PC running at its top performance. The **Check Disk** tool scans the hard drive for damage, both physical and logical. The **Disk Defragmenter** locates fragmented files and folders on local drives and puts the pieces together in one place. **Disk Cleanup** lets you get rid of unnecessary files and makes the most of the hard disk space. This tool lets you decide which unwanted files to remove.

As time goes by and you fill your computer's hard disk with music, videos and files, you may notice it becomes noticeably slower. This is often the reason why people "upgrade" their computer's hardware, by adding more memory or hard disk space. Upgrading hardware, as well as fixing hardware failures such as malfunctioning hard disks and power supplies, is considered non-routine maintenance and an experienced specialist technician should be consulted.

Unwanted programs can be deleted via the **Control Panel**, but additionally you should check your **Documents** folder for unwanted files and remove them, probably on a weekly basis, but at least regularly.

☞ Manoeuvres

1. To locate the **Check Disk** tool, select **Start** button, **All Programs**, **Accessories**, **System Tools** and finally **Disk Cleanup**.

2. Depending on your setup, a **Disk Cleanup Options** message may be displayed. If this is the case, select **My files only**.

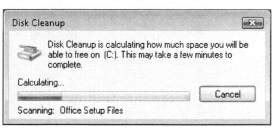

3. This tool calculates how much space can be freed and then displays the results. Decide which files you want to remove by checking the appropriate boxes.

continued over

Driving Lesson 65 - Continued

4. Click **OK**, then **Delete Files** to run the process.

5. To start the defragmenter, select **Start** button, **All Programs**, **Accessories**, **System Tools** and finally **Disk Defragmenter**. If a permission message is displayed, click **Continue**.

6. Make sure that no other programs are running and that any screen saver is turned off. Defragmentation takes a long time, so it might be best to perform this task when you have something else to do. If you want to go ahead, click **Defragment disk**.

continued over

Driving Lesson 65 - Continued

7. By default the defragmenter is run on a weekly schedule. This can be changed by clicking the **Configure schedule** button in the **Disk Defragmenter** window. Click **Close** to end the defragmentation process.

8. To check the hard disk for errors, open **Computer** window and right click on the hard disk icon, then select **Properties**. Display the **Tools** tab.

9. Click **Check Now**.

10. Click **Start**. Click **Schedule disk check**. The next time the computer is started this check will be performed. Close any open windows.

11. Unwanted programs should only be deleted if you are <u>absolutely certain</u> they are no longer required. To do this, open the **Control Panel** and click **Uninstall a program** under **Programs**. Currently installed programs are displayed. Select the program to be removed and click **Uninstall**.

Driving Lesson 66 - Cleaning Hardware

▣ Park and Read

It's important to routinely clean your computer hardware to maintain functionality and appearance. General cleaning instructions are given below, but you may need to refer to the manufacturer's documentation; remember to always dispose of cleaning materials safely.

Screen

Clean with the appropriate wipes - do not press hard on TFT screens. For laptop screens, a wipe with a damp (not wet) cloth is enough. Be careful not to get any liquid into the computer parts.

Keyboard

Unplug the keyboard and turn it upside down. Shake to remove crumbs, dust, etc. Spray between the keys with compressed air. Clean the keys with a mild cleaning agent or rubbing alcohol - don't use too much liquid. Let the keyboard dry and then plug it in.

Mouse

Unplug the mouse, dampen a paper towel with a mild cleaning agent and wipe the top and bottom. This is enough for an optical mouse. If the mouse has a ball, remove the cover on the underneath and remove fluff/dust from the rollers inside. Clean the wheels with cleaning agent; take the dust/fluff off the ball and run it under water. Dry thoroughly and replace in the mouse.

Case

Turn the computer off and unplug it. Outside: dampen a paper towel with a mild cleaning agent and wipe the case down - don't use too much liquid. Inside: remove the casing. Use compressed air to clean dust out of the vents and fan in the back. Use short bursts of air, blowing in one direction, to clean circuit boards, drives, etc. Replace the case.

CD/DVD Drive

Open the drive and blow compressed air into it. To prevent introducing dust into the drive, make sure disks are clean before inserting them.

Driving Lesson 67 - Dealing with Problems

▣ Park and Read

In the course of using a computer you will come across various error messages in dialog boxes, e.g. a program has stopped responding, storage facilities are full, there's a paper jam in the printer, you've lost a network connection, or your computer has been threatened by a virus. Error messages are designed to grab your attention, explain what the problem is and to suggest possible solutions.

There are various courses of action you can take to deal with these problems; *Windows* generally gives some guidance in the message boxes. For example, if a program has stopped responding there is an option to **End Now** - *Windows* will try to recover any work in programs such as *Word* or *Excel*. If you get a message that storage is full when you're saving work, try to get rid of any unwanted data (see Driving Lesson 65 on **Maintaining Systems**) and then try saving again - you could always save temporarily on to a memory stick while trying to resolve this problem. If you see an error message regarding a paper jam, try to clear the jam to remove the message (see the Driving Lesson 36 on **Printer Maintenance**). Should a lost network connection message appear, check any physical connections, i.e. wires; if it's a wireless connection, make sure the wireless box is switched on and working correctly. Any messages regarding virus threats will normally originate from your anti-virus software - sometimes it is simply informing you that an attempt to access your computer has been blocked. Carefully read any options given before taking any action.

If you don't know what action to take to deal with a problem, you must ask someone who may be able to help. There are various sources of help available to you: help menus included in the program; manufacturer's guidelines; experienced colleagues.

In some situations, however, you may need to get expert advice; perhaps from your IT administrator, a technician, or a help line. You will need to know how to deal with the advice you are given and be prepared to provide them with information. For example, they will need to know exactly what error message has appeared, with a reference number if one is shown. You may need to tell them what type of computer you are using and which operating system. If you call a help line, they may talk you through the process to resolve the problem. Follow their advice to the letter and if you don't understand, ask them to repeat the instructions. If you feel you don't have the skills to do what you are advised, then say so and find someone who can take over and help you work through the instructions.

Driving Lesson 68 - Revision

This Driving Lesson covers the features introduced in this section. Try not to refer to the previous Driving Lessons while completing it.

1. Why should you perform routine maintenance?

2. Name 2 ways to get rid of unwanted files.

3. How would you clean an optical mouse?

4. List some sources of help when problems are encountered.

[i] *Answers to this revision exercise can be found at the end of this guide.*

If you experienced any difficulty completing this exercise, refer back to the Driving Lessons in this section. Then redo the Revision Exercise.

Once you are confident with the features, complete the Record of Achievement Matrix referring to the section at the end of the guide. Only when competent move on to the next Section.

Section 9
Health & Safety
Environment

By the end of this Section you should be able to:

Identify Health & Safety Issues

Understand how to help protect the Environment

To gain an understanding of the above features, work through the **Driving Lessons** in this **Section**.

For each **Driving Lesson**, read the **Park and Read** instructions, without touching the keyboard, then work through the numbered steps of the **Manoeuvres** on the computer. Complete the **Revision Exercise(s)** at the end of the section to test your knowledge.

Driving Lesson 69 - Health and Safety

▣ Park and Read

Ergonomics

The term **ergonomics** refers to the relationship between workers and their working environment. The following aspects of the working environment should be taken into account when assessing whether or not a working environment is suitable for computer operation and whether or not it conforms to legislation:

- Provision of adequate lighting

- Provision of adequate ventilation

- VDUs appropriately positioned with screens free from flicker and interference and images free from glare

- Provision of monitor filters/anti-glare screens if required

- Suitability and adjustability of chair to provide the prescribed posture for the user, i.e. feet on the floor and a comfortable height in relation to the desk

- Provision of a mouse mat or suitable equivalent surface

- Suitably positioned keyboard, not too far away from the user

- Provision for frequent breaks away from the computer (10mins after every 50mins work).

It is an employer's responsibility to ensure that appropriate provisions are made available, but the employee has a responsibility to ensure that he/she makes use of them and goes about their job in an appropriate manner. They should make sure they take regular breaks, but also stretch their arms and legs from time to time while at the desk. They should also make time to relax their eyes when working with the computer. A workplace that has swivel chairs with adjustable positions, stable, roomy desks, etc. will provide a working environment that is comfortable and safe. If a computer, desk and chair are correctly positioned, they will help the user to maintain a good posture. Furniture and equipment needs to be suitably positioned, appropriate to the type of work for which it is intended and to conform to the relevant Health and Safety at Work (HASAW) legislation.

Lighting must be adequate to work comfortably, particularly if it is necessary to read documents whilst working. Positioning of light must be arranged so as not to cause glare reflection on the screen or distraction directly behind it. Artificial lighting can cause its own problems, and efforts should be made to provide natural light where possible, or good quality artificial light which attempts to reproduce natural light characteristics.

continued over

Driving Lesson 69 - Continued

Health Issues

Injuries common in an IT environment are:

- Aches and pains (especially to the **back**) due to bad posture when seated for long periods

- Repetitive strain injury (**RSI**) caused by poor ergonomics combined with repeated movements of the same joints, e.g. **wrist**, over a long period of time

- **Eye strain** which can be caused by **glare** or flickering from a VDU and by not taking regular visual breaks (10 minutes every hour is recommended) away from the screen

- Injuries due to tripping over trailing wires or other obstructions.

Precautions

In any work environment you must recognise that there are risks associated with using IT. Make sure:

- you take care when handling equipment, especially when moving or carrying heavy items

- the hardware and electrical items you use have been safety checked

- there are no trailing or **insecure power leads** or other cables

- there are no worn or frayed power leads

- there are no **overloaded power points**.

You need to know the relevant guidelines and procedures for the safe and secure use of IT in your organisation and, in any work environment, your employer must display the health and safety policy in a prominent place. Make sure you know where the policy is in your place of work. You can find up to date information on health and safety laws and guidelines that specifically affect the use of IT on the web site of the Health and Safety Executive **www.hse.gov.uk**. The relevant law is the **Health and Safety (Display Screen Equipment) Regulations 1992**.

The Environment

IT equipment and consumables must be disposed of correctly and safely. Some components such as monitors, batteries, wiring and toner cartridges contain chemicals which are harmful to the environment. Broken computers, monitors, etc. cannot just be disposed of with normal waste; they must be taken to a special facility for safe dismantling/recycling. Cleaning materials must also be disposed of responsibly.

continued over

Driving Lesson 69 - Continued

It is also desirable that certain steps be taken in an IT workplace to minimise the effect of working practices on the environment.

♦ Where possible **recycle waste paper**

♦ Where possible **recycle ink/toner cartridges** from printers and copiers

♦ Where possible use energy efficient monitors with **low power** options

♦ Use PC settings that enable "sleep" (or **standby**) mode for HDDs and monitors when the devices are inactive

♦ Where possible save documents in an electronic format within the computer system rather than printing out hard copies.

Manoeuvres

1. How would you ensure that your **working environment** was safe?

2. As an employee, what are your responsibilities towards your own **safety** in the workplace?

3. What precautions could you take to minimise the effect of your work on the environment?

Driving Lesson 70 - Revision

This Driving Lesson covers the features introduced in this section. Try not to refer to the preceding Driving Lessons while completing it.

1.   What is meant by **HASAW**?

2.   Describe a **good working environment** relevant to PC use.

3.   What is **RSI**?

4.   Describe some **Health and Safety precautions** which should be taken when working with computers.

5.   What **common injuries** might occur in such an environment?

6.   What do you understand by the term **ergonomics**?

7.   What two things can you do to save paper?

If you experienced any difficulty completing this exercise, refer back to the Driving Lessons in this section. Then redo the Revision Exercise.

Once you are confident with the features, complete the Record of Achievement Matrix referring to the section at the end of the guide. Only when competent move on to the next Section.

Section 10
Security

By the end of this Section you should be able to:

Understand the need for Backing up Data

Know about Privacy Issues

Understand the Information Security Issues

Understand Safe and Proper Practice

Understand Copyright Legislation

Know about the Data Protection Act

To gain an understanding of the above features, work through the **Driving Lessons** in this **Section**.

For each **Driving Lesson**, read the **Park and Read** instructions, without touching the keyboard, then work through the numbered steps of the **Manoeuvres** on the computer. Complete the **Revision Exercise(s)** at the end of the section to test your knowledge.

Driving Lesson 71 - Security Issues

🅿 Park and Read

Backing Up

In an earlier section, the fact that certain parts of a PCs memory are only temporary was discussed. It is, therefore, good practice to save your work to permanent storage (HDD or file server) after regular, short periods. This ensures that if a power cut occurs, only the data produced since the last save is lost. Certain software applications perform this task automatically.

Apart from protecting data against loss due to power failure, an organisation needs to consider the possibility of total file loss due to: a serious hardware fault, physical damage to the computer (possibly as a result of fire), infection by computer virus, theft or other malicious action.

The loss of vital files may be inconvenient to an individual using a home PC for hobby purposes, but to a business user, large or small, the loss could well be catastrophic. It is, therefore, essential for strategies to be available that enable regular, complete copies to be made of all files which are identified as being critical to an organisation. This is known as **backing up** files and may be carried out hourly, daily, weekly or in any combination thereof. Regular backing up ensures that even in the event of a total loss of data, an organisation has an almost current, duplicate set of its most important files, which it can rely upon to maintain business continuity.

Storage containing the backed up material is known as **backing store** and should be treated as a very valuable commodity. The fundamental reason for backing up files is to ensure that they cannot be lost, or completely destroyed, while saved on the hard drive of the PC or the file server. It is, therefore, not totally secure to keep the backing store in the same room, or even building, as the source material because of the risk of fire.

For absolute security, the backing store should be removed from the working environment (off site) and more than one set of backing store media should be used in rotation. All backup media should be kept in a storage environment, which is theft-proof, fireproof and waterproof.

continued over

Driving Lesson 71 - Continued

For an individual home PC user, such sophisticated techniques are unnecessary; however some backing up should be carried out. Always try to bear in mind how much time and effort would be lost if your PC either switched itself off or blew up! If the former happened, you would lose all unsaved work, if the latter, you would lose all work saved onto your HDD as well as all application software installed on your machine. It is good practice to keep all the original media on which application software is supplied, i.e. program CDs, in a safe place.

It is highly likely that at some point, for whatever reason, you will need to re-install application software. You should also make a point of backing up all files that you have created yourself and saved to disk.

Privacy Issues

If there is any need to consider the content of certain files as being sensitive or confidential, the use of password protection should be used to prevent unauthorised persons accessing, viewing or editing the data. A **password** typically acts as a user's **personal** entry code to their own PC, software or files and would usually be chosen by the user and never divulged to anyone. A perfect password will consist of a combination of letters and numbers and be of an adequate length, e.g. 8 characters, not just 3. Don't use something too simple like your name, date of birth or your dog's name. You should <u>never</u> share a password, or for that matter a PIN number, with another person. **Passwords** should be changed regularly, to prevent the possibility of misuse by unauthorised individuals.

As well as **password** protection, most organisations or systems would require the use of a **user ID** (otherwise referred to as a **user-name** or **log-in name**.) This is another level of access code that provides evidence of a user's entitlement to access certain areas of a network or system. A **user ID** would typically be assigned to users by the relevant organisation, i.e. the owner / administrator of the system or network in question. A number of users might be given the same **user** ID. This would identify to the system the fact that the user could legitimately claim access to the network, also, it would identify the level of access to which the user was entitled. The **password** would also be necessary to identify the individual user, and provide evidence of their entitlement to access their own files, within an area of the network designated as "theirs". *See information on **Authentication**, **Identification** and **Authorisation** later in this Driving Lesson.*

continued over

Driving Lesson 71 - Continued

It is feasible therefore, <u>if full use is made of password protection facilities</u>, for the following security measures to be in place when a user starts up a networked PC:

- ♦ A **password** must be typed in to gain access to the PC.

- ♦ A **user ID** must be typed in to gain access to the network or system.

- ♦ A **password** must be entered to gain access to shared directory space on the network server.

- ♦ A **password** must be typed in to gain access to a file saved in that directory space.

- ♦ A **password** must be typed in to gain authority to amend the file content by saving changes.

The different levels of access given by different **user ID**s are known as **access rights**. It is important that organisations have security policies in place with regard to **access rights**, in order that only appropriate personnel have access to the system and only appropriate personnel have access to sensitive parts of the system. These security precautions should be taken on top of normal, sensible, physical security measures such as burglar alarms, locks and keys, etc.

There are three processes that are activated when a user logs on to a computer system: **Authentication**, **Identification** and **Authorisation**. Authentication is simply the process to find out if someone is who they are, i.e. on computer networks authentication is carried out by checking log on user passwords. The process of identification connects the information you have given in your user name and password and checks that it matches the details held for you. Once you've been authenticated and identified, then the authorisation process checks if you have the required permissions to access the content. This is a bit like the computer saying, "I know who you are, now I'm checking what you're allowed to do."

Information Security

This term is used to describe methods for ensuring that data stored on a computer system is protected against being compromised, or against unauthorised access. It is important that any organisation should have an **active** policy to ensure that security is not compromised, rather than waiting to deal with any breach once it has happened.

continued over

Driving Lesson 71 - Continued

An **information security policy** should document such issues as:

- The details of a **user ID/password** policy as described above
- The **personnel responsible** for each level of security
- **Anti-virus** measures
- Penalties for **breaching security policy**
- Procedures for **reporting security incidents**
- Procedures for educating staff about their **responsibilities** regarding **information security**

As part of overall security consciousness, individuals should be aware of the sensitive nature of information stored in portable appliances such as **laptops**, **PDAs** and **mobile phones**. If such a device was lost or **stolen**, not only could **confidential files** fall into the wrong hands but personal information (**addresses, phone numbers**, etc.) could be misused by the finder and **contact details** could be lost to the company. All such devices should be kept safe at all times and password protection should be applied wherever available, also, as much of the material as possible should be included in any **backup** regime.

Manoeuvres

1.　Why is it good practice to **regularly save** to permanent storage?

2.　Why should at least one set of **backing store** media be kept **off site**?

3.　Describe the possible levels of **password protection** that may be applied to networked files.

Driving Lesson 72 - Safe and Proper Practice

◩ Park and Read

When using ICT based communication you need to know how to keep personal information safe but, equally, you need to respect the privacy and data of other people.

Personal Data

You can protect your data by using a user name and password and, on a more physical level, you can lock your computer and hardware with a security cable. When using the Internet, you must make sure you protect personal information. When making purchases on the Internet it will usually be necessary to supply financial data (usually credit or debit card details) to the seller. This process involves some risk (although probably no more than supplying the same details over the telephone) and so there are protection methods available to make the process safer. Making online financial transactions with a bank or insurance company for example carry the same level of risk.

Many web sites cannot be accessed without a user name and password; these are called protected sites. Sometimes you have to pay a fee up front before you can access a web site, which can then be done by entering the user name and password allocated to you. You will usually need a user name and password to shop online at supermarkets such as Sainsbury's or Tesco, and to use online financial services. Most sites that involve supplying sensitive financial data, e.g. shopping and banking sites, will be set up as secure sites. This means that all transferred information will be automatically encrypted (scrambled).

These web pages can be identified by **https** at the start of the **URL**, and a small padlock symbol, 🔒, on the **Status Bar**. Always ensure that you are using a secure site before supplying any financial or other sensitive information. Take as much care with your personal details on the Internet as you would in other areas of your life. Do not send financial details unless you are sure of the site and secure access is in force. Only e-mail such information if you are very sure you know where it is going. Always think before giving out details such as name, address and telephone number. This is particularly true in social situations such as e-mail correspondence and chat room activities. It is relatively easy to ignore someone electronically by deleting their e-mails or staying away from a chat room, but not so easy if they have your real name, address and telephone number.

continued over

Driving Lesson 72 - Continued

Respect for Others

It's very important to respect other ICT users and indeed their data. Plagiarism, the practice of copying the work of someone else and passing it off as your own, is a growing problem because of the sheer amount of information available on the Internet. It's very easy to copy and paste an essay or some other document - you must not do this. Always acknowledge your sources and be aware of copyright issues. This also applies to misuse of images - you must not use any images in your own work that are subject to copyright.

You must handle confidential information responsibly - make sure it is protected and dealt with in an appropriate manner. For example, don't leave a confidential document open on your computer while you go for a coffee break, and don't leave a CD containing personal names and addresses on the bus!

Be careful about the type of language you use. Although e-mail is often considered a less formal means of communication than other methods you must still make sure your language in not offensive or inappropriate. Before using e-mail, familiarise yourself with the rules of netiquette - network etiquette. Always use accurate and brief subjects in the appropriate field on a message. Keep your messages brief and relevant rather than rambling. Make sure your outgoing messages are spelled correctly and don't write in capitals - it's considered the same as shouting.

When forwarding or addressing messages to several recipients, be discriminating in your use of copy lists. If you use the **Cc** feature, all recipients will be able to see other recipients' e-mail address. Sometimes the **Bcc** feature may be more appropriate, where addresses are kept hidden.

Check the Internet use and e-mail policies in your organisation and make sure you abide by them.

Driving Lesson 73 - Copyright

P Park and Read

Software copyright legislation

Copyright protects creative or artistic works. Software copyright legislation exists to give the authors/developers of software the same legal protection as the authors of published, written and musical works already enjoy. The software legislation is, if anything, more restrictive in practice than traditional copyright laws. If an individual purchases a book or music CD, copyright law prohibits them from copying that material in any way, without the express permission of the author or publisher. They are, however, able to lend their copy of the book or CD to a third party.

Software copyright operates in such a way that an individual who buys a computer program, be it a game, a piece of application software or an operating system, does not actually purchase that item but purchases the right to use it within a specific set of criteria. It is a **single user licence** that has been purchased, allowing the user to install one copy of the software on a single computer on which the program will be run, together with the right to create one backup copy of the software (unless specifically excluded). The licence details accompanying the software will also set out exactly what the user is permitted to do with it without contravening copyright laws.

Due to the widespread use of laptops and other portable PCs, some software licences allow the software to be installed on two machines as long as they are not both used simultaneously. This recognises that more and more users have a desktop PC in their office, as well as a laptop that they carry around, or a desktop machine at home. These users will need to run the same software on both machines and as (in theory) they cannot use two machines at the same time, they are not forced to buy two expensive copies of the same software.

However, unlike a book or an audio CD, a piece of software cannot be loaned to a third party, since that would presumably mean that an unlawful installation of the program would have to be made in order for that third party to run it.

Files and copyright issues

The ready availability of **Internet** access and of **multi-media input/output devices** such as **digital cameras** and **scanners** raises important issues relating to the copyright status of files, such as music files, images and so on. Basically, any **image**, **text file**, **music file** or **video file**, unless created by, written by, composed or filmed by the user is protected by internationally recognised copyright legislation. <u>This means that no copy, either in paper form or digital format, of any type of material, may be created without the permission of the owner of the copyright.</u>

continued over

Driving Lesson 73 - Continued

The copyright owner is deemed to be the author/creator of the original item, or, in the case of an organisation, the employer of the author/creator.

The effect of this legislation is that **any** text or picture **scanned** into a PC and saved; any **image**, **text file**, **music** or **video file** downloaded from the Internet and saved to disk is **illegal**, unless specifically identified by its owner as being **copyright-free**. This situation also applies to any digital material saved on **removable media** such as **memory sticks** and **CD/DVD**s. This material must be considered to be copyright protected unless distributed by its owner, or specifically identified as being **copyright-free**. Effectively, therefore, it should not be **used or distributed**!

Software Licenses

As discussed earlier, a typical piece of software is sold with a **single user licence**, allowing only one installation of the software to be carried out. In order to cater for the situation within an organisation where a software application is used by all employees, multi-user **site licences** can be purchased. Any licence would have to cover the likely maximum number of users. The penalties for infringement of software copyright laws can be very severe indeed!

When a piece of software is installed on a computer, there is usually a point in the installation process where the user has to enter their own name and/or their company name. There is another stage when the user has to signify (usually by ticking a check box) that they have read and accepted the **End User Agreement**. This is the document mentioned earlier, which details exactly what the user is permitted to do with the software. The **End User Agreement** is usually displayed in a scrolling dialog box at the same stage as the indication of acceptance by the user. Without this acceptance, installation will not proceed.

Product ID

Once a legitimate software installation has been completed, the details you have entered are locked to that application. Each individual example of the program has its own **registration number** known as the **Product ID**. It is possible to view this information to check that this version of the software is licensed to a particular person. The information is displayed by selecting the **File** tab then **Help**.

The required information is shown on the right.

continued over

Driving Lesson 73 - Continued

Shareware is a type of software that can be obtained on the equivalent of a sale-or-return basis. The software is obtained and distributed free of charge and installed for a pre-determined trial period, typically 30 days. At the end of this evaluation period, the software is programmed either to cease operating, or to flash up reminders, unless a payment is made to the author/software house.

Another type of shareware is software that is available free of initial fee, but is not the fully functioning version of the program. The watered down version allows the potential of the package to be evaluated, but the operator must then pay to receive the full version, together with registration and technical support as an official user. The main advantage of shareware is its cost. Relative to major commercial packages, useful software can be acquired extremely cheaply, often in the £10-£30 price range.

Freeware is, as the term implies, available completely free of any purchase or licensing fee. It is provided by programmers, who write software for their own interest and are then prepared to make the fruits of their labours available to others. Shareware can originate from a similar source, but the author presumably has decided to recoup some reward for his/her efforts.

Open Source software provides the source code for the software under a licence, allowing users to change and improve the software; they can then redistribute it.

Manoeuvres

1.   What does the purchase of a **single-user licence** allow a software user to do?

2.   Discuss some pros and cons of using **shareware/freeware**.

Driving Lesson 74 - The Data Protection Act

🅿 Park and Read

The **Data Protection Act (1998)** regulates the use of personal data by all businesses. It aims to promote high standards in the handling of personal information, and so to protect the individual's right to privacy. This act defines personal data as any data that can be used to identify a living individual, including names, addresses, personalised e-mail addresses and video images of such individuals, e.g. medical records, employee records.

Data Controller

Under the Data Protection Act (1998), a person who determines the purposes for which and the manner in which any personal data is to be processed, is the **data controller**. In a business that is not run by a sole trader, or that is not a partnership, the business itself is defined as the data controller.

The law requires data controllers to give their details to the **Information Commissioner's Office** for inclusion in a public register, unless their data processing is exempt. This is so that people can find out who is processing personal data about them and why they are doing so.

The Act sets out eight rules that data controllers must follow for protecting personal data; these are known as the eight principles. Personal data must be:

- ◆ Obtained and processed fairly and lawfully.

- ◆ Processed only for one or more specified and lawful purposes.

- ◆ Adequate, relevant and not excessive for those purposes.

- ◆ Accurate and kept up to date.

- ◆ Kept for no longer than is necessary for the purposes for which it is being processed.

- ◆ Processed in line with the rights of the individual.

- ◆ Secure and protected against loss, damage and inappropriate processing.

- ◆ Not transferred to countries outside the European Economic Area unless there is adequate protection for the information.

continued over

Driving Lesson 74 - Continued

If a business does not comply with the principles, the Information Commissioner can take enforcement action against the data controller, whether it is an individual or a business.

Data Subject

This is the individual who has data kept about them. The data subject has the right:

- to be informed when information is being held

- to be told the purpose for which it is held

- to know to whom the data will be disclosed

- to refuse to allow their details to be used for direct marketing.

☞ Manoeuvres

1.   What type of information is covered by the **Data Protection Act**?

2.   Describe the **Data Protection Principles**.

Driving Lesson 75 - Revision

This Driving Lesson covers the features introduced in this section. Try not to refer to the preceding Driving Lessons while completing it.

1.   What does **backing store** mean and why is it important?

2.   How can **unauthorised access** to computer file systems be prevented?

3.   What can happen to **data and files** in the event of a power cut?

4.   What is the difference between a **User ID** and a **Password**?

5.   What do you understand by the term **access rights**?

6.   Detail four issues that an effective **Information Security Policy** should set out.

7.   How can a **computer virus** enter a system?

8.   Name three different types of **virus**.

9.   Explain the difference between a **virus** and a **bug**.

10. Why is it important to update **anti-virus** software on a regular basis?

11. What do you understand by the term **software copyright**?

12. How do **shareware** and **freeware** differ from mainstream software?

13. Why may it be illegal to distribute images which have been downloaded from an unknown source on removable media?

14. Give an overview of the implications of the **Data Protection Act** for computer users.

If you experienced any difficulty completing the Revision, refer back to the Driving Lessons in this section. Then redo the Revision.

Once you are confident with the features, complete the Record of Achievement Matrix referring to the section at the end of the guide.

Answers

Please note: these are example answers only.

Driving Lesson 14

Step 2   Double click (with the left mouse button)

Step 3   A window

Driving Lesson 31

Step 10   The **Modified** date is shown as 17 February 1993.

Step 11   **Cam.docx**.

Driving Lesson 32

Step 1   **Marketing**, a *PowerPoint* presentation.

Step 6   16 files

Step 7   18 files.

Driving Lesson 37

Step 2   This will vary between computers.

Step 3   In the **Printers** window either
Select the printer and click the **Set as default** button
Or
right click the printer icon and select the **Set as Default Printer** option.

Step 8   This will vary between computers.

Step 10   You might need to align print cartridges after installing or replacing a cartridge, if printed characters are not properly formed, if the margins are misaligned or if straight lines look wavy.

Driving Lesson 52

Step 4   **Revision.zip** is 430KB, **2 Managing Files** folder is 750KB. These sizes are approximate. They will depend on exactly which exercises have been completed.

Driving Lesson 56

Step 1   False. They can totally destroy data.

Step 2   False. Any computer can be infected.

Step 3   True.

Step 4   True.

Step 5   True.

Step 6   False. They can lie dormant.

Step 7   False. Many applications will remove viruses.

Step 8   True.

Step 9   False. It needs to be updated on a regular basis.

Step 10   True.

Step 11   Possible costs of having a virus in the system include:

Before detection, the virus could cause poor computer performance, system crashes, etc.

Once detected, computers will be out of action until the virus is dealt with.

External consultants employed to remove virus.

Re-keying any lost data.

Fraudulent transactions due to security breaches.

Apologising to any customers, contacts, etc. who may have been inadvertently infected with the virus before it was detected.

Driving Lesson 64

Step 5   It reverts to the original setting.

Step 6   The **Preview** button.

Step 9   Increase the resolution and the icons will look smaller (and vice versa).

Step 11   a) Volume slider in Media Player

b) System Volume control on the Taskbar

c) Volume control on speakers

Driving Lesson 68

Step 1   Routine maintenance should be performed to keep your computer healthy and running at peak performance.

Step 2   Use the **Disk Cleanup** tool or delete the files yourself on a regular basis.

Step 3   Clean an optical mouse by simply wiping thoroughly with a paper towel dampened with a mild cleaning agent.

Step 4   Sources of help: help menus, manufacturers' manuals, IT admin, technicians, colleagues, help lines.

Driving Lesson 69

Step 1   You would make sure your workplace was safe by checking for: trailing or insecure power leads or cables, worn or frayed power leads, overloaded power points.

Step 2   An employee is responsible for making proper use of provisions and going about their job in a responsible manner.

Step 3   To protect the environment you could recycle waste paper, ink and toner cartridges, use monitors with low power options and PCs with standby mode. You could also save documents rather than print out hard copies.

Driving Lesson 70

Step 1   **HASAW** is Health and Safety at Work.

Step 2   A good working environment would be well lit and ventilated, have glare free VDUs, adjustable chairs and mouse mats provided. There would be provision for breaks from the computer.

Step 3   **RSI** is repetitive strain injury.

Step 4   Check for: trailing or insecure power leads or cables, worn or frayed power leads, overloaded power points. Make sure your chair is at the correct angle for your back and your feet touch the floor, that your monitor screen is free from glare and you have regular breaks.

Step 5   Some common injuries: back ache due to poor posture, RSI, eye strain and trips or falls.

Step 6   **Ergonomics** means the relationship between workers and their environment.

Step 7   To save paper you can recycle it and save files to disk rather than print them.

Driving Lesson 71

Step 1   You should regularly save to permanent storage in case the computer crashes, there is a power failure, or there is some physical, permanent damage to the computer.

Step 2   At least one set of backing store media should be kept off site because of the risk of fire, theft or flood.

Step 3   Possible levels of password protection for networked files: a password to access the PC, a user ID to access the network, a password to access the directory or network server, a password to access the file, a password to amend the file content.

Driving Lesson 73

Step 1   A single user licence allows the software to be installed only once.

Step 2   Advantages of shareware/freeware: either cheaper than major commercial packages or totally free. Disadvantages: shareware is either a not fully functioning version of the software, or will shut down after a trial period unless a fee is paid.

Driving Lesson 74

Step 1   Personal information, e.g. names, addresses, financial information, etc. is covered by the Data Protection Act.

Step 2   The Data Protection Principles are conventions that must be followed by all organisations keeping information.

Driving Lesson 75

Step 1   Backing store is storage containing backed up material and is important because it may be needed due to computer failure, damage, etc.

Step 2   Unauthorised access to files can be prevented by applying passwords to every level of access.

Step 3   In the event of a power cut any changes made to data and files since they were last saved may be lost.

Step 4   A user ID lets the system know that the user is entitled to access the network and also which level of access is allowed. A password is a user's personal entry code to a computer, software or files.

Step 5   Access rights are the different levels of access allowed by different user IDs.

Step 6   Any four of the following: details of a user ID/password; the personnel responsible for each level of security; anti-virus measures specified by the security policy; penalties for breaching security policy; procedures for reporting security incidents; procedures for educating staff about their responsibilities relating to information security.

Step 7   A virus can enter a system through an e-mail attachment, floppy disk, CD or DVD, or the Internet.

Step 8   Any three of the following: time bomb/logic bomb, macro virus, worm, Trojan Horse.

Step 9   A virus is a malicious piece of programming intended to cause harm, but a bug is an error or fault in a piece of software code.

Step 10 Anti-virus software should be regularly updated because new viruses appear every day.

Step 11 Software copyright gives authors and developers of software the same legal protection as authors of published, written and musical works.

Step 12 Shareware and freeware are cheaper than mainstream software (or free). Shareware often has a free trial period or a trial of a cut down version of the program, before the fee is payable.

Step 13 This material must be considered copyright protected and it is therefore illegal to distribute it.

Step 14 For data holders, the Data Protection Act means they must ensure the data is secure and disclosed only for legitimate purposes. They must only hold relevant material and nothing more. The data must be accurate and up to date and not held when it is no longer needed. The information must also be accessible to the individual concerned.

Glossary

Application	A stand-alone piece of software which can be used for a specific purpose.
Archive	A file containing one or more compressed files.
Autorun	A program on a CD, DVD or floppy disk which starts running as soon as the disk is loaded.
Backing up	Making copies of all important files
Compact Disk Drive	A device used to read and write to and from Compact Disks.
Compact Disk	Also known as CD's, these contain hundreds of megabytes of information.
Compress	Use special software to save a file or group of files so that they take up much less space.
Computer Virus	A malicious piece of code which can cause damage to computerised systems.
Control Panel	An area on the computer from which the user can perform advanced administrative tasks.
Desktop	The first display screen of *Windows* from which all other applications are run.
Drivers	Software which enables an application to use a specific hardware device, e.g. printer.
Firewall	A filter to control traffic from your PC to the Internet and vice versa.
Floppy Disk Drive	A device used to hold, add and remove data from 3.5inch floppy disks.
Floppy Disk	A small capacity external storage device.
Folder	A method of grouping together files (and other folders).
Formatting (text)	Changing the appearance of text. Any text from a single word to a whole document can be formatted.
Hard Drive	Also known as HDD, the Hard Drive is a large storage medium on which files can be saved.
Hardware	Any physical part of a computer system.
Icon	A small visual representation of an application.
Keyboard	An input device used to enter text into a computer.
Monitor	A visual display unit used to show the user information about what the computer is doing.

Mouse	An input device which is used to control the cursor on the **Desktop** area of the computer screen.
Multimedia	An application or function that involves many techniques such as text, sound and video.
Multiple Selection	Selecting several files and/or folders from a display so that an action can be applied to all of them.
Notepad	A basic text editing application supplied with *Windows*.
Power Switch	A switch usually found on the front of the system unit which supplies power to the computer.
Print Preview	Allows a user to see on screen how a document will look when printed.
Print Queue	A list of print requests waiting to be processed by a printer.
Read-only	A property given to a file or folder which means that it cannot be amended.
Recycle Bin	An area of storage where deleted files are held temporarily before being deleted completely.
Shortcut	An icon (usually found on the **Desktop** area) which opens an application stored elsewhere.
Subfolder	A folder that is contained within another folder.
Taskbar	By default, a blue bar running the length of the **Desktop**, at the bottom of the screen. Shows which tasks the computer is performing.
Wizard	A program that guides a user through a complex task by asking a series of questions.
Zipping	Another name for compressing a file.

Index

Record of Achievement Matrix

This Matrix is to be used to measure your progress while working through the guide. This is a learning reinforcement process, you judge when you are competent.

Tick boxes are provided for each feature. 1 is for no knowledge, 2 some knowledge and 3 is for competent. A section is only complete when column 3 is completed for all parts of the section.

For details on sitting ECDL Examinations in your country please contact the local ECDL Licensee or visit the European Computer Driving Licence Foundation Limited web site at http://www.ecdl.org.

Tick the Relevant Boxes **1**: No Knowledge   **2**: Some Knowledge   **3**: Competent

Section	No.	Driving Lesson	1	2	3
1 Getting Started	1	Preparation			
	2	Starting the Computer			
	3	The Windows Desktop			
	4	Arranging Icons			
	5	The Taskbar			
	6	The Start Menu			
	7	Opening Windows			
	8	Sizing and Moving Windows			
	9	Close a Window			
	10	Scroll Bars			
	11	System Properties			
	12	Using Help			
	13	Shut Down and Restart			
2 Managing Files	15	File Storage			
	16	Folders and Files			
	17	Navigation			
	18	File Types			
	19	Sorting File Displays			
	20	Creating New Folders			
	21	Copying Files and Folders			
	22	Moving Files and Folders			
	23	Selecting Multiple Files			
	24	Viewing Object Properties			
	25	Renaming Files and Folders			
	26	Deleting Files and Folders			
	27	The Recycle Bin			
	28	Copy a Floppy Disk			
	20	Searching for Files/Folder			
	30	Advanced Searching			
3 Print Management	33	Printers			
	34	Add a New Printer			
	35	Print Jobs			
	36	Printer Maintenance			

Tick the Relevant Boxes **1**: No Knowledge **2**: Some Knowledge **3**: Competent

Section	No.	Driving Lesson	1	2	3
4 Running Applications	38	Run an Application			
	39	Entering and Formatting Text			
	40	Saving Text			
	41	Print a Document			
	42	Using Print Screen			
	43	Switch Between Applications			
	44	Closing an Application			
	45	Install/Uninstall an Application			
	46	Create Desktop Icons			
	47	Use Desktop Icons			
5 Using Compress	49	File Compression			
	50	Compress Files			
	51	Uncompress Files			
6 Virus Control	52	Computer Viruses			
	53	Anti-Virus Protection			
	54	Anti-Virus Protection Applications			
7 The Control Panel	57	Control Panel			
	58	Date and Time			
	59	Display Options			
	60	Screen Saver			
	61	Background and Resolution			
	62	Colour			
	63	Sound			
8 System Maintenance	65	Maintaining Systems			
	66	Cleaning Hardware			
	67	Dealing with Problems			
9 Health and Safety	69	Health and Safety			
10 System Maintenance	71	Security Issues			
	72	Safe and Proper Protection			
	73	Copyright			
	74	Data Protection Act			